This is an inspiring read and re
settle for mediocrity or believe
down. She reminds us that life is for living and it belongs to
us to do what we believe in!

Sarah Lemon – CEO, Beauty Therapist, Lemon Zest Skin &
Body Therapy

I feel a range of emotions. It made me sad, cry, but I could
actually feel your drive and passion to make the most out of
your life and that life is so precious.

Vicky Bryson – CEO, Therapist, Blue Ash Reflexology

Wow! Anita, it's so well written. You feel like you are actually
there. I had smiles, tears and real emotions at the surface. You
should be proud of what you have achieved, accomplished
and been through.

Shiene Mann – CEO, Beauty Therapist, Touched by an Angel

Anita, you're 'no ordinary girl'. You are 'extraordinary!'

To tell your story is so brave. I found it an honest, from
the heart read. To have faced so many challenges in your life
and to tackle each and every one of them with such courage,
determination and a deep desire to achieve your dreams, is
both heartwarming and inspirational.

Rachel Long

Anita writes with such enthusiasm and passion of her journey
from quiet retiring girl to a successful confident business
woman.

The book aims to encourage and motivate anyone who is thinking of setting up their own business, and this is achieved in bucket loads all the way through her story.

A riveting read.

Lin Griffiths

Sometimes you meet someone and know that your paths have crossed for a reason. This is how I felt after reading Anita Swetman's first book. I loved the energy and positivity which Anita provokes in her readers. I love how her dreams unfold and nothing stands in her way. There is strength and power, ambition, hard work and passion which I identified with and made reading her book such a joy. If you don't know where to start and have doubts in your life, this is definitely a book to read. It will inspire you to never give up on your dreams.

Lisa @CrazyFoxyRetreats

Absolutely loved this book! What a true inspiration Anita is! If you are looking for the courage and determination to go after your dreams, then this is the book for you! Anita has overcome so much through her life, and with great determination she has proved that you can achieve anything you want if you are determined enough. Her courage knows no bounds, it is very well written and also very informative, and at times heart-rending! But an absolute must read!

Kerry Bodill

"Your father would have been so proud of you!"

Sylvia – Anita's Mother

No Ordinary Girl

A true story

Anita Swetman

To Kerry
You are free to be
whatever you want to be!
Anita

First Published by Fuzzy Flamingo 2022
www.fuzzyflamingo.co.uk

ISBN: 978-1-7397850-0-0

Editing and design by Fuzzy Flamingo
www.fuzzyflamingo.co.uk

Author photo 2021 Siobhan Elizabeth Photography MPA

A catalogue for this book is available from the British Library.

Disclaimer

My book is intended to help and inspire you with my story for you to reach out for your dreams and let nothing or no one hold you back. In certain chapters of my book, I make suggestions to help you on your journey and your well-being. I am not offering any medical advice and if you are worried at all you must seek professional help from a medical practitioner.

To Gary, Kieran and Kirsty
My rocks

In loving memory
Dad, Stephen and my dear friend

Dad, I hope I have made you proud x

"Being brave isn't the absence of fear. Being brave is having that fear but finding a way through it."

Bear Grylls

Contents

'There are no limits, only what you go and give yourself.'

Anita Swetman

About the Author

Anita, who lives in Warwickshire with her husband, is described as a kind, caring and calm lady, who has strong positivity and determination to help other people.

She is a very proud stepmother to two amazing children and is also a national-multi-gold-award-winning beauty therapist and massage therapist to A-listers.

When Anita is not busy in treatments with her clients, hard at work with continual professional development or writing, she can often be found out walking round her lovely village or spending quality time with family and friends.

Her mission is to reach out to everyone who wants to change their direction in life but lacks the self-belief. You are worthy of becoming the person you want to be, and you can have the career you dream of, even if you don't know where to start the change.

You too have the power within yourself to change the course of your future.

CHAPTER ONE

The wake-up call

"Oh my goodness, what happened? Is she all right?" I heard a voice faintly in the distance. I still don't know how I managed to avoid all the obstacles on the floor without causing further damage to what had already happened to my face as I found out when I returned to consciousness. I lay still on the floor, dazed, unaware of what had just happened to me. I remember one of my favourite songs was playing on the radio. 'It's a Beautiful Day'. I heard the words so clearly as I came to on the floor; at this point I was still unaware of what had just happened.

My face felt numb, I was so, so cold. I was in a state of shock! Where was I? Was I dreaming? I just couldn't focus on anything other than the feeling of, well, absolutely nothing down the side of my face. "What happened? Where am I?"

"Just look at your eye!" my colleague gasped. It was black and blue and closing up by the minute.

It was in August 2003, I was getting married to my soulmate in a months' time, and was so excited about my big day. We had been planning the event for over a year! This could not be happening to me. But it had. As I lay there on the floor with all eyes on me, what had just happened?

When I came to, my colleague said that I had fainted and hit my head on the floor. One minute I was sitting on the chair, the next I was slowly coming to next to the radio that lay beside me on the floor. As I slowly sat up, in an instant it suddenly dawned on me why this had happened. My inner voice was calling out to me. The stress of the workload was getting far too much for me, I just couldn't do this anymore. It was as if my body and soul had said it had had enough and I collapsed. The last thing I remember before the incident, I was talking to my manager about what work was expected that week, then the next moment I was gone.

The thing is, as I look back now, it was probably the best thing that had ever happened to me. "What?!" I hear you ask. Yes, it was, because it was a wake-up call. If I had kept doing what I was doing, running myself ragged, I knew I would never make it to old age. Stress can do strange things to your mind and body; if you don't watch the signs, you will get wiped out by a boulder like I did. I learned the hard way.

★

It was a warm, overcast day in September, the best day of my life. I had dreamt about our special day for so long and had put so much into the planning. The day itself itself had all gone smoothly. I had visualised exactly how our big day would go. I felt like the luckiest woman alive, saying my wedding vows in front of close friends and immediate family. I wish my dad could have seen me say 'I do'. The whole event felt surreal, as I had gone over and over in my mind how it was going to be.

You see, never in a million years did I ever expect to meet and marry such a wonderful, loving, loyal, caring person. I didn't feel worthy to be a wife or even a stepmother.

"But why, Anita?"

As my story continues, you will see and understand, and maybe even resonate with it, if you are my ideal reader.

★

I had still felt numbness around my left eye and, luckily, I only had a very tiny black mark under it, which I managed to conceal, but every time I look at my wedding photos, I can still see the mark, that constant reminder of the pain of what had happened that day at work. Even if no one else could see anything, it reminds me of my moment. That moment I subconsciously made the decision to change my life. My wake-up call. But how? How was I going to change my life? At this point in time, I did not yet know.

I went back to work after our wedding and carried on with my duties as normal until the following January in 2004, when a friend lost her daughter suddenly on New Year's Day. She was more or less the same age as I was, so young and full of life! I just couldn't believe that someone so young had been taken away from this world, just like that! Everyone I knew was shocked and no one could believe that she had died so suddenly with no warning. It scared me and made me realise once again how short life can be.

It was a few days later when I experienced a dream, a vision so strong. It was of me, being the proud owner of my own salon. But I was a pharmacy technician working for a well-known pharmacy chain. I had no knowledge of being a beauty therapist or running a business. I had studied business studies at school when I was fifteen, but I had no business degree! So, I dismissed it. But the dream, the vision kept coming back to me night after night, getting stronger as if I could actually feel and see myself in a new career. I could no longer ignore it; a higher purpose was definitely guiding me towards a different path. But, what should I actually do about this vision, this dream?

It wasn't until a year later, in early 2005 – that's how long it took for me to actually build up the courage to look into what it would entail to become a beauty therapist. A whole year! Because I was afraid, I feared the unknown. When I had been in the same career for so long, I felt like I wanted things to change, but didn't have the courage to make that leap of faith and move forward to do something about it! I kept procrastinating, putting things off. I just didn't know how to get to where I wanted to be, so I just took it one step at a time.

The first step in changing my career was to tell myself that I could do this! I am capable of going in a different direction, as my destiny is not set in stone.

I needed to look into what options there were to study at college and gain the necessary qualifications and experience to get to where I wanted to be. I saw our local college was having an open day, so it was the perfect place to begin my search. I stood in line at thirty-two years of age, amongst all the sixteen and seventeen year olds who were excited to do the same courses that I was looking into at the college.

I thought, 'Why am I here? I must be going mad! Me? A mature student! I'm not seventeen anymore, it's too late to go back to studying!' These were the words I kept saying to myself over and over. It's funny how, when I look back to that day, something so strong was pushing me in the direction of the lecturers and there I was standing in that queue. I could feel the young students' eyes burning into me from all round the room. Or was it all in my imagination? I can't even begin to tell you how scared I felt. I just wanted the ground to swallow me up! I wanted to turn back and run away. I was trying to talk myself out of going into the main hall and, instead, go back to my car! But, as I turned around in the queue, I saw so many people behind me, I couldn't just walk out now, everyone would look at me! So, I froze. I didn't move until I was called over. "Too late now!" I said to myself. But was it? I felt so foolish afterwards because I'd had a lovely chat with the lecturers discussing what my aim was for the end of my course, as well as the options to study first to become a fully qualified beauty therapist and then my options on further courses after I had qualified. I did not realise how many opportunities there were out there in this field of work. The possibilities were endless! So much to take in. It was a real eye opener into the leisure and well-being industry. So different to the medical industry.

I went home armed with all my college information and, after sleeping on it, I knew that this was the right path for me. The next day, I enrolled onto my first course, which was a year-long level two diploma, part-time, just two evenings a week at the college as well as home study, portfolio building and practicals. I went home and proudly said to my husband, "I did it."

I slept so much better that night, so proud of myself that I had taken that first leap of faith to enrol onto my course. I didn't take out any loans, I just used some of my hard-earned wages to pay for it. It felt right. I trusted my heart.

Now what I needed to do was to work out how I was going to actually fit college into my full-time career! That was my next challenge. Oh and of course I needed to speak to my boss. That scared me even more than standing in line at college! Can you imagine the scenario?

To my relief, my manager was actually very understanding, as he knew that my accident at work had changed me and I wanted to do more in life, so he agreed to allow me to reduce my hours slightly on the days I went to college. Only by a couple of hours, but it was enough time for me to prepare for my studies.

I felt so relieved. The tension left my body, as I had been so worried that I wouldn't be allowed – be allowed! How silly is that?! To have to ask permission to go back to college to study whilst still in my present career!

But that's how it is in a career. A job. You are not the boss; you have to ask permission for everything you do! Holidays, time off, how much you earn, days, hours worked… Your life is not your own.

I was pleasantly surprised to find I was worrying over nothing. But if I hadn't plucked up the courage to TELL my boss that I was planning to go back to college as a mature student and ASK to reduce my hours then I would never have got them!

So, always remember: If you don't ask, you don't get! Be brave, as you are not stuck where you are, no matter what the voices in your mind, or other people, tell you.

I could have avoided asking, thinking to myself 'he will say no'. What would that have achieved? Absolutely nothing. I would remain stuck in my rut.

Some of my friends and colleagues were pleased for me, and some were shocked. Others didn't say anything. But you only have one life, you need to do what is right and fulfilling for you. No one else. This is YOUR life!

In September 2005, I proudly commenced my college course. But this time as a mature student (wiser, I might add).

On my first day, I met the rest of my class for the very first time. I thought it would be just like going back to school as I sat there with the other students of different ages and backgrounds. We each in turn said who we were and what we did in our lives, what we wanted to get out of the course, as well as career progression. I felt like I had been given a second chance. My time to make a significant difference in my life. The thing was, when I was a girl at school, I was always frightened to put my hand up in class to give the answer in case I got it wrong and looked stupid. So, I would sit quietly and say nothing at all, scared of what others thought about me. I was a prisoner in my own body, but now I was starting to come out of my shell at the age of thirty-two! I even had my bridesmaids all go in the registry office in front of me when I got married, so all the attention would be on them and not me! Even in front of my family and closest friends, I was just so scared. A frightened girl. I had hidden it so well that no one knew. I did manage to tell the whole class about myself, but it was very hard, I was shaking like a leaf! But I did it.

I was pleasantly surprised to see some of the students were of the same age as I was, and some were older! Yes, older than I was. One of those students became one of my best friends. We are still close friends to this day. And by the way, my friend who was the oldest in the class won the student of the year award! I was so proud of her. "Show off your achievements," I would say to her. But she wanted it kept quiet. She didn't want to shout out about it. But why keep quiet about such an amazing accomplishment? To win an award, an accolade, is such a big thing and should never be kept quiet.

"Stand tall. Be proud of what you have achieved and the person you are becoming."

Anita Swetman

I can say this quote now, but at that moment in time I admit I had to agree with her.

I was surprised at how much I loved college. I always went into class with a spring in my step and made some new friends too. I never wanted to leave as I was having such a great time with my newfound love of studying different therapies and treatments. I spent my other evenings at home studying and building my portfolio instead of watching TV. I was finding a way. I stayed focused and was getting on with what needed to be done to hit my goal. I became really involved in the practical and theory work, plus it helped to take my mind off my daytime career in pharmacy. I wished I had done this years ago! But I hadn't had the vision, the dream. I wouldn't have believed in myself that I could do it prior to this.

'It's better to start something later in your life, than not at all and live to regret it."

Anita Swetman

I had been bullied at junior and high school. My dad had kept me wrapped up in cotton wool. He always tried to protect me from the bad things going on in the world, but I thank him so much for doing this because it has made me the strong, ambitious woman I am today. I had always been ambitious but scared. Scared of the unknown. I wanted to go to a famous academy in London when I was seventeen to learn hairdressing but I was told I would never get in there! I believed what I had been told, so I never pursued it. I didn't believe I could do it, and others had said the same. So, they must be right! Weren't they?

I truly believe everything happens for a reason at the right time in your life. Everything I believed up to this point was showing me my path and, at this point, I was still unaware of where it would lead me. But there were lots of challenges along the way, too. The coursework was tough, it's not just painting nails! It was so tough studying at college, studying at home, building my portfolio, deadlines, working my full-time job plus making sure I didn't forget my husband and family in pursuit of my dream. Some people just didn't understand why I wanted to change my 'safe' career. They never said anything to me, but I could tell by the look on their faces!

I had saved up hard from my wages and went without things to pay for my college course, as it wasn't cheap. But somehow, deep inside my heart, I knew I was doing the right thing.

By the time it came to the end of the year, half the class had quit, and I had developed duodenitis, and was in such pain in my stomach. The stress of it all was eating away inside of me. My life seemed to be hanging by a thread. I just didn't know if I could go on anymore. It was exam time and the pressure of college, work, plus the exams were really taking their toll on my health. But was it worth it? Yes, as I graduated and received my diploma with a distinction. The fire in my belly was so strong. I had envisioned it and backed it with action! Nothing was going to stand in my way of achieving my first goal of finishing my first year at college.

"If you can visualise it, you can achieve it, but you must back it with action."

Anthony Robbins

I shocked everyone! Especially my colleagues and my family. So now what? Okay, so I have a level two diploma, what is the next step? I hadn't a clue. I was exhausted.

My husband and I went on holiday to the Greek islands a couple of months after I graduated. I did heal and started to relax, but I just couldn't switch off. The education bug was so strong in my system, I was hungry for more. It's funny, when I was at school, I never really paid too much attention in some of my subjects. Why? Because I had a learning difficulty with maths. A learning difficulty with maths and I became a pharmacy technician? The teacher used to say to me, 'Go sit down and work it out for yourself.' That was how I discovered my learning difficulties. I didn't manage to work the problems out for myself. Hence, I got unclassified in my GCSE for maths. It was only because I had a patient pharmacy tutor that I passed my pharmacy maths exams. I am forever grateful for their support. But it was never my calling to practise pharmacy. I loved working with my colleagues and customers, but I always had a holistic approach in life to healing. This was how I was brought up, it was in my blood, running through my veins, deep inside.

"Don't let your past dictate who you are, but let it be part of who you will become."

Louis Mandylor

CHAPTER TWO

Don't be scared

In 1991 I lost my dad.

I was only eighteen. He was no longer in this world. I had my family, but I had to face life and live on my own. I no longer had my shadow to protect me from harm. I felt so lost. A part of me had died that day, too.

I used to hide behind my dad, I was so afraid, so scared of life. He used to wrap his little girl in cotton wool to protect her from harm. He thought he was doing the right thing. So, when he was no longer there to protect me, I just didn't know what to do. How could I go on living on my own?

So, I became the protector. Looking after my family. I took all the focus off myself to avoid the pain I was feeling deep inside.

"I'm so scared! I can't do this anymore!" my inner voice would say. But it was okay to be scared. It was okay to be afraid. I did eventually learn how I could go on and live a fulfilling life without my dad. But that was years ahead.

That day, the day I watched my dad fight for his breath

and leave this world right in front of my eyes, was one of the hardest days of my life. Nightmares haunted me for years. I went in and out of depression and would cry myself to sleep. No one knew, I never told a soul. What had happened that night in the bathroom of our family home was an experience I will never forget. He hadn't been well that day, he'd broken down in his van on the motorway and had been very stressed, his breathing was getting worse. He used his medication, but nothing seemed to work. I was upstairs when my mum shouted at me to come down. I ignored her as usual, being an ignorant teenager, but then the screams were so loud I could no longer ignore them. "GET DOWNSTAIRS NOW!!" I knew then that it was serious. I bolted down the stairs, but it felt like I was going in slow motion. I had never heard my mum shout like that before, adrenaline started to rush through me. My heart was pounding so loud I could actually hear it. The nightmare of what I was about to witness haunted me for so many years afterwards, witnessing my dad sitting in the bathroom going blue in the face, fighting for his breath. He then fell onto the floor. It all happened so quickly, yet it was as if it wasn't happening at all. Part of me was refusing to believe what I was seeing. Both my brothers were there, too, but only my older brother Steve and I saw the horror of what had just happened. My brother kept pumping his chest trying to get our dad to start breathing again. It seemed like forever until the ambulance arrived, then the doctor arrived afterwards. I crumpled into a heap on the floor. Everything was moving in slow motion, I was screaming! I couldn't even begin to describe how I felt at that moment, I had just died inside.

The ambulance crew fought hard to save my dad, but he died a couple of hours later at the hospital. He had hung on for so long. I know now my dad would never have wanted to survive this ordeal, as his brain had been starved of oxygen. He would not have wanted to carry on living like that, so he left this world at peace with himself.

Remember, remember the 5th of November. How can I forget? I'm reminded of it every year! The night I lost my shadow, my dad, forever.

It was after this major event in my life that I started working in my pharmacy career. I needed to do something with my lost life, so I got a job working in the chemist where I had worked since I was a Saturday girl at fourteen years old. My manager gave me support to study, which meant I could do distance learning whilst at work. I worked and studied hard for my NVQ as a pharmacy technician, I was making excellent progress and achieving over 90% for my coursework. I even went for a week to summer school at Sunderland University, which was an event in itself! Me, go to university? I never ever would have dreamed that would be possible. I got unclassified in maths! But I did it! I went to university, and I was so proud of myself. But I would never do things alone. I always had to have someone with me. As if I needed looking after, I guess. I was so afraid. The pain, the emotions were all deep inside, all locked away. My dad had done his best to protect me from this world.

When he was gone, I was left a scared, frightened little girl. I won't ever blame my shadow because he thought he was doing the right thing for me. There were no rules or books on how to bring up your children, you just did what you thought was right for your child. My dad thought he was doing what what was best for me.

But it is because of how I was brought up that I am the strong woman that I am today.

I CHOSE not to stay a frightened little girl. I CHOSE to grow as a person into believing that if I put my mind to it, and backed it with action, I could achieve whatever I believed.

"All the magic happens outside of your comfort zone, and in order to get that magic, you have to change."

John Lee Dumas

CHAPTER THREE

The power of positive thinking

When I was twenty-three, my older brother Steve introduced me to a business opportunity. I was so excited to be in the main banquet hall at a local luxury hotel. I was surrounded by all these excited, positive people who were dressed in business attire. I had never been in this kind of environment before, where you couldn't help but be drawn into the uplifting atmosphere. It was all so alien to me, but I found I really did like it!

But what was I doing here? How did I end up here? It was way beyond anything I had experienced before. I was quite comfortable working in my job and moving towards gaining my NVQ, but something inside said to me to go and check it out. I had nothing to lose, after all, it was a free to view opportunity. My dad had always been self-employed since we were children and he always had different businesses on the go. Window cleaning, plumbing, painting and decorating, door-to-door product selling, chimney sweeping, even fixing up old cars and selling them on! He was also in a band touring the country in his youth! That was how he met my mum. My dad was very entrepreneurial, open minded and a perfectionist. A master at his craft.

I remember when I filled out my marriage certificate forms, when the registrar asked what my father did for a living when he was alive, I automatically replied, "Well, actually, he did everything!" I was looked at very strangely. My dad had never kept his eggs all in one basket, he knew that you needed to have multiple forms of income just in case one ever gets taken away from you. I understand that now as I write my memoir, but at the time I hadn't a clue what it meant.

My brother had said to me, "Anita, just come along with an open mind and listen to what they have to say." That was it! I was so caught up in the excitement and I felt the best I ever had! My mood lifted, and I was feeling so good for the first time since I had lost my dad. This positive thinking stuff was very contagious and was a whole new concept to me, so I signed up to the free network marketing opportunity.

This was it! This was my time, my moment. I was all fired up, started to make a few sales and recruited my first team member. I had even started to develop a positive frame of mind with all the motivational books I read and all the tapes I listened to; there were so many, and I have a couple of favourites that I still refer to today. 'You can do this! You are worthy' and so many other quotes like this were becoming IMPRINTED on my subconscious mind, and it also shone in my work in pharmacy, as I started to feel so much better about myself.

A year later, I quit! I didn't take the network marketing opportunity any further. I quit because I didn't truly believe in myself. I didn't believe I was worthy of success. I truly was scared. So scared I threw up! I kept thinking about the success and what I could achieve, but as soon as I had made a few sales I then went on to talk myself out of them! "Why would they want to buy from me?" I look back now at how I used to be, a frightened, nervous little girl! But this was all part of my learning curve. The student wasn't ready. When will the student ever be ready? I kept thinking about what could have been. Why I quit. It just wasn't for me, this wasn't what I wanted to do, running my own business. I had no business degree and no knowledge of running a business, even though they were teaching you all you needed to know and, in fact, the concept of duplication and launching a business was so simple! I just couldn't do it. I had no faith or belief in myself. But what I learned with all the positive thinking books and motivational tapes whilst I was involved in this business opportunity had led me subconsciously to where I am today, writing this book for you. I never learned the power of positive thinking to succeed in life and business in business studies at school, I wish it had been on the curriculum.

I have so much to be thankful for, though, as that business opportunity and positive mental attitude helped me to gain a better career in pharmacy, as I applied for a position with a very well-known chemist chain close to where I lived. It offered better money, prospects and fewer hours than I was doing at the time. My new career also led me to meet the man who stole my heart, whom I went on to marry. If I hadn't made that decision to change my direction in life, I would never have met my husband.

"You are one decision away from a completely different life."

Mel Robbins

CHAPTER FOUR

I quit!

I look back now as I write my memoir and I can't believe that I quit! Having said that, if I could go back in time, would I have done anything differently? "You should have been braver, you should have looked fear in the face and defeated it!" NO! I actually wouldn't change a single thing! Because it was all experience. Experience of life! Because, at that point, when I was in network marketing, I had absolutely no belief in myself. But – and a BIG BUT! – it led me to gaining a better career path where I worked my way up with hard work, persistence and studying to finally becoming a Registered Pharmacy Technician. This is a professional status, and I was very, very proud to achieve this.

I carried on in that role for the next twenty-three years of my life! Even though it wasn't my calling, I threw myself into my work and it led me to meet the love of my life. If I had chosen a different career back then, I would have gone down a completely different path, so NO! I wouldn't change a thing. My path was part of great things that were still yet to come. Life and success are always a journey. Whether you choose to follow the signs is totally up to you. If I hadn't fainted and hit my head, I wouldn't have had the vision of what I wanted to achieve in my future. I chose to trust my vision. If I hadn't taken the leap of faith, I would still be working in that career, waiting for my life to change. It took me a very long time to realise that the only person that could change my life was me! The only regret I did have, however, was that I took so long to go for it as I procrastinated. I kept putting things off, I didn't feel worthy of success. Why shouldn't you chase your dream? You only have one life! I kept thinking about my vision and what it was trying to tell me. Fears, doubts, I didn't feel worthy or good enough.

We all have hopes and dreams, they are gifts that are given to each and every one of us. It's the little voice inside your head that tells you that dreams are just dreams and are not achievable. Your inner voice that tells you that you are not good enough. You may have had other people say to you that it's all a dream and you will never achieve your vision.

I always looked at other successful people and thought, 'It's all right for them, they've made it! They are the exceptional ones!' What did I find out? They are not exceptional. They are normal people, just like you and I, who fought through their negative voice, all of the negative people who laughed or told them it was impossible and trusted their gut and went for their dream!

It's not all a bed of roses in making something of your

life. It takes hard work, dedication, determination and a mental toughness to go the distance. You have to have the guts and gumption to get out there to do what it takes to become a success at anything in your life. But how will you know if you are ready? Trust me. You will never be ready. You just have to dive into that ocean. Trust that it is your path and that you will be able to do whatever it takes. Winners find a way! Keep on keeping on and never ever quit!

If we wait until we are 'ready', we will wait for the rest of our lives! Don't wait! The time is now! Don't ever put things off, as you never know what hand you may get dealt next. If you're not sure what you want to do in your life and feel stuck where you are, then I suggest the best place to start would be to look at what your interests are in life. Do you have any hobbies? Not sure if you could turn your hobby into an income? Maybe you could visit your local library and start at A and go right through to Z. Go onto Google! What grabs your interest?

You will need to also look at positive motivational books, as there are so many to choose from to help you grow as a person too. It's a great place to start and then, once you find the possibility of a new career, you can look into what it will take to get to where you want to be. Join Facebook groups with like-minded people who will inspire and help spur you on. Keep an eye out for groups in your area you could attend. I can't guarantee success, but you stand a very good chance of changing your life. Just take it one step at a time and believe you can do it.

★

When I quit, it wasn't the business opportunity that I had quit on, it was myself. But something inside wasn't giving up. I'd always had that spark. That spark that was inside of me just waiting to be ignited again. Unfortunately, that didn't happen until 2004. From 1996, it was a very long time for a spark to stay there; it was dimly lit but it never, ever went out. For me, it was always one step forward and three steps back! You are aiming for three steps forward and only one step back to reach your goal. Keep on keeping on, and never, ever give up on your dream. It takes as long as it takes… never give up on yourself.

★

Who says that YOU aren't good enough? Your friends, family, yourself? No one was telling me I wasn't good enough; it was *me* telling *myself* I wasn't good enough. As I meditate, writing my memoir, I look back in my heart yet again, deep into my past, and I realise just how much time I had wasted waiting until I was ready to take that leap of faith to go back to college. I found out the hard way that I just wasn't ready and would never have been. I just had to go and do it! The time is now! Don't wait. Tomorrow is not promised. Yesterday has gone. This minute, the time is now!

After I graduated from college in 2006 with the education bug burning through my body, I then went on to study further whilst I was still working in pharmacy. I decided on Swedish Body Massage, as well as advanced facials and hot stone therapy, which I completed in 2007. My newfound love of holistic therapy was in fact already deep within me, coming up to the surface, as I moved closer to fulfilling my dream. Then, as if I didn't need any more challenges in my life, it happened yet again…

CHAPTER FIVE

Things happen in your life to test you

"Hey sis! I'm going into labour! Don't you worry about me, you both go and have a wonderful weekend away." My husband and I were just on our way out of the door when I received the call. I was so excited I was going to be an auntie again.

We had no phone reception where we were staying, so I didn't know what had happened whilst we were gone.

It was September 2008. Having experienced the perfect textbook pregnancy, absolutely no problems whatsoever, we were all so happy to be welcoming this child into the world. But this was not to be. She came into our world and fought bravely for her life for two days. I could have lost my baby sister too, thank goodness she survived. It was another moment in my history that I will never forget. I was supposed to be taking a few days off to celebrate and help my sis with her first born, not going to her baby's funeral and consoling her! This could not be happening. I couldn't even begin to imagine what they were going through, I felt numb. Inconsolable.

When I went back to work, my manager had said it was like I was grieving my own child. I experienced headaches, anger, I would snap at people without realising what I'd done. I would go home and cry to myself silently. No one knew. No one knew the pain I was in; it was as if something had died inside me once more.

The funeral had been heart-breaking. So many people had come along to see the tiny coffin, which held such a brave child. This child I felt such a deep connection to. My dear niece. It was as if she was my own. She had hung on for a whole two days. Two days in this world but, if she had survived, she would have been 95% brain damaged. They had to make the painful, heart-breaking decision to turn off the life support machine that had been keeping her alive. Inconsolable. The family was in total disbelief.

It was not long after the funeral that I started experiencing more health issues. I made an appointment with my GP to discuss my ongoing headaches and the way I had been feeling. I sat in the waiting room thinking everyone was looking at me. But they weren't, I was *thinking* they were, I know it was all in my imagination as I sat there. What was I doing here? I wanted to run away. Far away from everything, from life itself. As I sat there in my doctor's office, pouring out my heart with my ailments, it was then as if, all of a sudden, something snapped inside. I broke down in sobs right in front of my GP! Embarrassing as I thought it was, this was it. This was my cry for help without even realising it. I was put on medication to help me to feel better and, after a few weeks, I did start to feel better as the serotonin levels in my brain were upped. But I knew medication wasn't the answer, as it was masking what was going on in my mind and deep within my heart. Why had I acted the way I had and grieved my sister's baby like it was my own? I needed answers and I wanted to find out why I acted and felt this way because something inside was telling me this wasn't right.

I visited my GP once again, saying I wanted to look into alternative therapy to get to the bottom of what was causing these feelings I was experiencing of grieving my niece as if she were my own child and ongoing headaches that had come upon me again. My GP suggested I try meditation and hypnotherapy. I was referred to a therapy centre to experience hypnotherapy for the very first time to see if it would work for me. I started to feel more positive, now that I was getting the real help that I needed instead of popping pills that were masking the underlying causes. Yes, medication did help initially, but it is not to be relied upon, in my opinion.

I met my lovely therapist who performed a thorough counselling session and then the treatment began. Hypnosis isn't about 'When I snap my fingers you will be cured' or 'You will do as I say', it's a deep connection into your subconscious. To bring to the surface what the root cause of your pain is. It takes time and persistence, and it was very painful bringing everything up to the surface to a complete stranger, but I highly recommend it. I also believe you should go on a recommendation of great reviews or through your GP to find the right therapy for you.

With regular weekly sessions, I started to heal from within. I began to feel more human. My headaches were easing, and my mood was more on an even keel. If ever you've experienced dark depression and got through it, or you are still experiencing it, you will understand what I mean. It was tough and I had to be open and honest with everything that had gone on in my life up to that point. I was grieving the loss of my niece to a certain extent, but it went deeper. With counselling, it came out that I was still grieving the loss of my dad from all those years ago! I had buried it so deep that it came pouring out of my soul. I had buried my sorrow so deep into my subconscious mind so that I could go on and live a 'normal' life. But it wasn't normal, I had been going in and out of depression for so many years and that is no way to live healthily. You must seek help and finding the right course of therapy may take time, but with persistence, and having that belief in yourself, with the right professional help, you too can be healed. Never suffer alone. Always reach out for professional advice and help.

My hypnotherapy sessions had helped me to be able to come to terms with my feelings. The hurt, anger, pain, the constant mood swings. It certainly explained why I had been suffering from headaches. I was like a coiled spring ready to explode! Well, I had, in front of my doctor. It was my subconscious calling for help. If I hadn't made the decision to have therapy, I can't even begin to imagine how my life would be now.

We all have decisions and a path to take in life; whether

they are right or wrong, you just don't know until you try.

I continued to have monthly hypnotherapy sessions until I no longer felt I needed them and it was after my healing had finished in early 2012 that my manager approached me and asked if I wanted to reduce my hours in pharmacy. I think a higher purpose had been watching over me, as I jumped with delight at the chance to be able to go down to working just three days a week so I could have some downtime. Little did I know there was yet another challenge just around the corner that made me finally make one of the biggest decisions in my career.

*

It was the summer of 2012. I went on holiday with my family to the beautiful Greek islands once again. Clear blue skies, sun every day. Fish mezes on the beach and cocktails every night. We had such a wonderful time, but on the flight home my health took a turn for the worst.

"Anita, wake up!" I could just about make out my husband's voice. My head felt like a balloon had blown up inside and the whole plane was spinning. Everything was muffled. It had all happened so suddenly. The last thing I remember was eating a peppermint as I was feeling thirsty. Then the next moment I was gone. I found I couldn't even stand up! I collapsed again. What was happening to me?

I couldn't fault the cabin crew on the flight, they made sure I was well looked after. We landed at Gatwick Airport and no one was allowed off the plane until the paramedics had examined me. They didn't know if they would have to quarantine the flight! Embarrassed was hardly the word I would use! I could feel all the eyes of that packed plane looking at me. If ever I have had a moment in my life where I just wanted to be swallowed up into the chair I was sitting in, this was it! But the state I was in, I was just too ill to care! The paramedics couldn't find anything 'physically' wrong with me, but I couldn't stand up straight, I had to keep my head lower than my heart as I was so dizzy. The whole plane was still spinning around in my head. I was carried off and through customs in a wheelchair. I couldn't stop vomiting. I had to close my eyes. I couldn't look at anyone as I could feel everyone's eyes burning into me, horrified with what they were seeing. What was wrong with me?

At our local hospital I had heart tests, blood tests, but nothing was found. My GP was puzzled, then he had a an idea that my condition could possibly be labyrinthitis and that I had experienced a severe attack of vertigo on the flight. I guess it would have explained what happened as there had been no other explanation. But it was because of this health scare that I finally took action! This was it!

Don't put off your dreams any longer, as you just don't know what is waiting for you around the corner.

On the 5th of November 2012, at long last I founded Tranquil Beauty. My little professional home therapy business. The day I finally launched my business was such an exciting day for me! I worked part-time for just two days a week around my pharmacy career. My vision from taking my newfound qualifications and college experience was finally happening. Better late than never. If only I hadn't left it so long.

But all I'd had was college experience. I had no idea how to actually get my business going. The clients don't just come to you, especially when you work from home, as no one knows you are there. I had no shop front, no passing trade. It was just me, my treatment couch and a few products I had purchased from the beauty wholesalers from when I was a student. What I did have was the vision and determination to make it a success. I would find a way. I believed I could do it.

I was so scared, I just didn't know what to do. I was building this new adventure in my life and all I did was trust my instincts that this was my path. I would find a way, and just kept on moving forward. My friend had shown me how to keep my account books and also set up a Facebook page to announce my new venture. My husband had helped me to convert our spare bedroom into a treatment room. I had some friends from work and a couple of neighbours who would come for a treatment, but that was it, not much business. I even put out lots of flyers around my neighbourhood advertising my new business. Leaflets through letterboxes. Nothing. No one booked in. Not one single person. Was this it? The beginning of the end? No! This was my dream, my vision! Why weren't people booking to experience a treatment with me? Why? What was wrong with me? I started to doubt myself. Could I do this? Could I make this a success? Was it that I didn't have any experience? Well, we all have to start somewhere to gain experience, so I carried on giving treatments to my few friends who booked in. I trusted the process and carried on building up my experience, and my faith and confidence in myself started to grow with each passing day. My light had started to shine. I even created my own website! There are some great ones that teach you how to build a very simple website yourself. It was brilliant to get myself up and running. This was now my shop window, showcasing all about me and my treatment offerings.

If it's going to be, it's up to me!

"Stop relying on other people, rely on yourself! Take responsibility for your life. Take responsibility! Be your own person."

Jerry Scriven

These words kept on ringing in my head. I had heard them many years ago when I was involved with network marketing. I knew I was meant to learn this positive thinking stuff!

Chapter Six

Strangers come into your life for a reason

When I used to work in pharmacy, I parked my car each day in a very convenient location only a ten-minute walk into town, down a side street to avoid the congestion of traffic in town. It was so wonderful to de-stress and have some exercise with the lovely walk into Stratford-upon-Avon along the river.

One day, a lady parked behind me and said to me, "Is it okay to park here?" I said, "Yes, of course, I walk in every day for work." She said, "Great! I work in town too, may I walk with you?"

I had made a new friend that day. We both looked forward to meeting each morning and walking into town together; there was always something to talk about! We laughed, we cried. As our friendship grew, we both started to open up to each other about everything going on in our lives on our walks into work every day. We found we shared a mutual history. It was strange, a bit surreal really. As our conversations got deeper, we discovered that both of our dads had died on exactly the same day, and they were both the same age of only fifty-four. How spooky is that? Was I meant to meet this person? I truly do feel that people come into your life for a reason. Trust your gut instinct. You will know if it feels right or not.

I had spoken to my friend about starting up my own business but not really getting very far with building it and that I was starting to lose faith in myself again. But I'd come this far, I couldn't give up now! With all my diplomas and certificates plus all the hours and dedication I put into my newfound craft, I could not let it go to waste.

"I have an idea that may help you. I can get you a stall to promote your business at our school Christmas fayre, which is coming up next week. Would you like me to reserve you a table?" My friend was on the school committee and had said it may be a great way to help promote my business. But I'd never done an event at a fayre before. I don't like being with crowds of people, I'm quite happy to stand back and hide. But I also knew that if I wanted to change some things that weren't working, I needed to look at other ways to see what would work. So, I threw caution to the wind and my heart was telling me to go for it; I had nothing to lose but absolutely everything to gain.

One Saturday in December 2012, just over a month after I started my business, I attended my first ever Christmas fayre at our local school. I woke up that morning after a very restless night worrying about what would happen at the event. But I tried my best to keep positive and envisioned it being a huge success with lots of new customers wanting to book in to experience treatments with me. I said to myself, "There's going to be a lot of mums here today!"

I arrived two hours early and I set up my table at the school with a pretty tablecloth, my business cards and treatment brochures, some products to sell, my diary and my nail lacquers. That was it! I decided that day to keep it simple so I could stay in control and keep calm. I was going to perform mini file and polishes at the event as well as promoting my services. This was the starting point of my new business and I found I gained a couple of new clients from this event. It was working! I had felt the fear and took myself out to meet the people and not wait for them to come to me. It was at the Christmas fayre that I also met the reverend of our local church. We got on so well and we got talking about a wonderful charity she supported, The Amasango School for street children in South Africa. It was at this point I had my very first light-bulb moment.

I thought to myself, "What if I performed a charity afternoon tea pamper event at the church? It would raise money for the charity and also help get my name out there too!" So, after much debate with myself, I decided not to put it off any longer and, with a lump in my throat and my heart beating hard in my chest, I nervously phoned the reverend the following weekend to discuss my ideas. We arranged a meeting, and this was where I also met the associate minister of the church. I remember serving up Earl Grey tea and shortbread to my guests as we chatted about all our ideas for the event that seemed to come together so well. I'm so glad I picked up that phone and didn't talk myself out of asking! It was as if it was meant to be. We set a date for around Mother's Day in March 2013 for a charity afternoon tea and pamper event at the church in our village. Now we had to get planning! I only had a couple of clients at this point. Once again, I thought to myself that I had absolutely nothing to lose and everything to gain.

It was very hard work bringing it all together successfully. I had decided to offer back massages as well as arm and hand massages for our guests. I asked one of my therapist friends whom I made great friends with at college to see if she wanted to help me with the treatments. I had said to her we would be working for free for the charity and in return I would give her a treatment to say thank you for helping me. The reverend was taking care of the planning and promoting of the event and the associate minister would organise the volunteers as well as cakes, sandwiches and ticket sales. I was in charge of organising my team, as well as pre-booking treatments. I had asked a couple of friends if they would help with reception work greeting our guests at the event. We all seemed to work together so well and the dream we had all envisioned for three months came true when the big day finally came.

I couldn't sleep the night before the event, I was feeling nervous as well as excited all at the same time! My stomach was churning, I knew I was well and truly coming out of my comfort zone to do something so different. "There's no backing out now," I said to myself, "you can't let all these ladies down! Everyone has worked so hard for this special day."

'Just do it, don't overthink it, you can do this! Go for it!' I must have heard those words somewhere before in all the motivational books I'd read, drumming it into my subconscious mind. They came into my conscious mind naturally as I got ready. I put on my professional uniform, and I was very well groomed. I stood in front of my tall mirror for a very long time, looking at myself and smiling, thinking how far I had come, yet still had so far to go.

The event was sold out! Treatments sold out! We had to turn people away! It ran so smoothly and was so well organised by the team of volunteers.

We'd had the most fun day, but we were all exhausted at the end. All the excitement and emotion of making sure it had gone smoothly certainly does wear you out. We had all given our time for free and it was worth it. We raised over £500 for the school; I was so so proud. I had taken the focus off myself to help others. This was when I realised I had found my calling. My calling was to help others in life. What if I had let the fear take over, and hadn't made the call to put forward my idea? I trusted my heart and I'm so glad I did. But little did I know what was just around the corner for me.

CHAPTER SEVEN

'Daring to be different'

'DARING TO BE DIFFERENT'. This was the heading for my very first article that went into our local newspaper. The editor wrote: 'It's never easy to start a new business, especially in the present financial climate, but Anita has taken the bold step. That bold step into the unknown. Anita has shunned a typical high street salon and started her business working from a dedicated room in her home.' The article also had links to my website and contact details.

I am still, to this day, heavily involved and dedicated to my clients in my business, and now I am booked weeks ahead. So different to when I first started with no clients whatsoever. The only experience I had was college and practice.

> "Never ever stop believing in yourself, you don't know what you are capable of until you try."
>
> *Anita Swetman*

In 2013, I had experienced my very first beauty show. It was at ExCel London. A massive exhibition of all things beauty and massage. I was so excited to talk to different companies and to network with other therapists about their businesses. I was a long way off from where these businesses were, but I enjoyed my day, but I enjoyed my day. It was at this event that I experienced my very first taster of a Lava Shell Massage. The world's first self-heating massage tool. I had trained in hot stone massage, but I didn't enjoy performing it very much. A stop-start massage, the stones were way too hot to pick up and massage with, it wasn't for me. So how could Lava Shell be any different? It was an amazing new technology. I took all the forms and went home to have a good think about it. I couldn't afford the training or the equipment but something deep inside was urging me to do this. I loved the treatment. It was so much better than hot stone, so I saved as much as I could from the small number of treatments I was performing for my clients to pay for the course and equipment I would need.

In October 2013, I trained to become a Lava Shell practitioner with the Lava Relax massage. A deep, relaxing holistic heated massage proven to be effective with helping depression, anxiety, insomnia plus it was heavenly to perform. I soon fell in love with this treatment and the few clients I had, wanted to experience my newfound craft. I asked one of my clients who had the massage from me if she could do a review for the *Wellesbourne News*. This article is what she wrote to the editor:

'I have been having treatment at Tranquil Beauty for a while now. Anita always greets you with a friendly smile and an offer of refreshments. You then go up to her treatment room, which has a wonderful aroma of oils. I have recently had my first Lava Shell Massage and Anita's professional approach in explaining the treatment helped me to understand how the Lava Shells would benefit me and how they worked. As I got comfortable on the couch, the treatment began. And wow! The penetration of heat transferred from the shells to every muscle in my body was wonderful. The whole treatment made me feel relaxed and gave me a great sense of well-being. I would recommend Lava Shell to everyone, so why don't you give it a try? You won't be disappointed. I guarantee you will want to go back to Tranquil Beauty.'

I was starting to get myself out there. Asking my client to post a review in return for a treatment in our local news was proving to be a success for me. More people were hearing about my amazing new massage and wanted to book in. I had fallen in love with my craft. I fell in love with the feeling I got when I had made a difference in someone's life after they experienced a treatment with me. This was it! It was really happening! My business was starting to finally take off, albeit slowly. Yes, people came, but only came once or twice. It wasn't a regular visit. "It was just a treat," they would say to me. My heart sank. How could I sustain a business on occasional clients? Would I have to stay in my pharmacy job forever? No! I was determined to make this work! I needed to find a way to have my clients coming back every single month!

"Remember, if it's going to be, it's all on my shoulders to make this work. No one else!"

Anita Swetman

It was in February 2014, only a few short months after I had trained in this amazing new massage, that I decided to train in the Lava Shell Therma Facial. A deeply holistic, meditative facial that zones you out to another world using natural mineral therapy skincare. One of my clients had booked in for this treatment with me one day after she had seen the Lava Shells live on *This Morning*. She said to me, "I saw the Lava Shells on TV and I've been telling all my friends that Anita does that treatment!"

It was at this point another light bulb had exploded in my head! Another vision. Could I do this?

CHAPTER EIGHT

Moving out of the comfort zone

It was only a week later when I received an email asking for therapists who wanted to become a Lava Angel. Lava Angels massage press, media and celebrities at events around the country, as well as in my own treatment room with our very own amazing Lava Shells.

The director wanted to increase publicity for the company and in return it could boost your own business, too, if you chose to do it. There were further opportunities for you to even organise your own events too!

My client's words were ringing in my head over and over. I just couldn't get them out of my mind. It was as if they were imprinted in my heart, which was pounding by the way!

"I saw the Lava Shells on TV and I've been telling all my friends that Anita performs this treatment!"

It was as if this email had been delivered specifically for me. I thought, "What if? What if I could massage celebrities and the media. That would really give the boost my business needs with what it could do to my reputation." My mind kept racing over and over, thinking about the possibilities that could lay ahead for me. But then my thoughts turned to: "You'll never get to do this, only the lucky, beautiful, successful therapists get to massage A-list people. Why would they choose me? HA HA! You're not worthy or good enough!"

I looked at myself in the mirror. I looked deep into my own eyes and then said out loud: "Why wouldn't they choose me? What makes me any different to anyone else who massages the media? I excel at my craft, my clients' reviews are telling me I am excellent with my massages. I can do this! YES, I CAN! YES, I CAN!"

It was at this point I decided I wasn't going to put this off any longer or else more doubts and fears would fill my head, and they had been coming in thick and fast, trying to talk me out of applying. I wouldn't have pursued it any further. The memory from so long ago about being told I wouldn't get into a famous hairdressing academy in London, which I believed back then, that I wasn't good enough to do things 'out of the ordinary' that people could do had entered my head.

My palms were sweating as I filled in the application form with shaking hands and then I placed a passport photo of myself to support my application. That afternoon, I had stood there looking at that postbox and hesitated for a long time with the brown, sealed envelope that was still in my hands. I was debating whether I should just tear it up and throw it in the bin. I threw caution to the wind and once again said to myself: "What exactly do you have to lose by doing this? Absolutely nothing!" So, I very quickly put the envelope into the postbox before I could talk myself out of it again. That monkey brain with negative thoughts telling you that you can't do things can be quite loud sometimes! Don't listen to it!

There, I'd done it! I felt proud of myself, but my stomach was churning over and over. That feeling is when you know you are starting to move out of your comfort zone because what you have done 'feels uncomfortable'.

I couldn't eat my dinner that night. My stomach was doing somersaults! I was so afraid of the unknown, of what could come of this. My negative voice had crept in once more, saying, "Don't worry, you won't get it anyway, so you may as well stop worrying." Those feelings of discomfort subsided as I was then talking myself out of being chosen, so I could quite happily go back into my little bubble of comfort. So, I slept soundly that night and forgot all about my application.

The next day, though, I saw a further email looking for Lava Angels. My stomach started churning up once again. Those little feelings of maybe, just maybe... This time I started to visualise being a Lava Angel with my famous Lava Shells at a big event. I could actually see myself performing in this role!

"I can do this, I will get through! I will become a Lava Angel!"

It was a further week before I heard back from the company. I saw my name on the email and very quickly opened it.

'Dear Anita,

I would like to invite you to come and work with us at Beauty UK at the NEC in Birmingham for the day…'

This was it! My chance had come. My chance to prove that I could do this! I was so excited, I was jumping around the room with delight! I had got through to the next stage of selection to work with the team to prove I could do it. I could become a celebrity massage therapist.

I rose bright and early that Sunday morning, after a restless night. I wanted to make sure I arrived early in case of traffic. Yet again, I very nearly didn't go. My negative voice was creeping in once again… "You won't get chosen, you're not good enough!" But I had to go, I couldn't back down now, they were expecting me!

I gave myself a very firm talking to as I looked at myself in my mirror. I had on my clean, pressed therapist uniform and my hair and makeup were immaculate. "You know you can do this! You stand exactly the same chance as anyone else who applies for the position."

I sat in my car in the car park of the NEC in Birmingham. What was I doing here? I felt so sick, and I had a nervous headache. I slowly started to calm down as I listened to positive, uplifting music on my CD player. What was I doing on my day off voluntarily working on a Sunday to see if I'm capable of massaging celebrities?! "That's why I am here! I can do this. Don't get scared now!"

I took a deep, calming breath and made my way to

the hall to meet the director of the Lava Shell team. It was 9.30am. The exhibition was due to open in thirty minutes, so I was given my instructions. This was finally it. No going back now!

My first job for the morning was to greet salon and spa owners into the exhibition and hand out flyers directing them to our stand. In my hand, I also had a heated Lava Shell, so I could show and tell people what Lava Shell was all about, and they could feel the heat from this wonderful, self-heating massage tool. I was so nervous, but I did start to relax and just be myself talking to others as if they were my own clients.

In the afternoon, I had the chance to work on the company stand with the team chatting to salon and spa owners about the products and services as well as performing massages on them in the massage chairs. The director was around most of the time, but I chose to pretend she wasn't there so I could concentrate on what I was doing and just be myself, building rapport with people.

It was the end of a long, nerve-racking, exhausting day when Clare came up to me and said, "I've been observing you all day and gathering feedback from the team. I love your personality and I would like to invite you to The Lava Party."

All I remember was shrieking, "YES PLEASE and THANK YOU!"

I had done it. I had officially become a Lava Angel.

CHAPTER NINE

Feel that fear and go for it!

It was July 2014, the big day had finally arrived! It had seemed like an eternity since I had been chosen to massage at my first ever celebrity event. I was up early that day to meet another Angel at a local railway station, as we were travelling together to go to a mystery location. Where were we going? It was my first time travelling into London without my husband, so I was glad I wasn't going on my own. I was so excited, nervous, afraid, wanting to throw up! Why was I putting myself through all this? It was the biggest turning point in my life so far and I'd come this far, now I had to see it through. I was pushing myself to the limit and going way out of my comfort zone! Besides, I couldn't let my colleague down and leave her to travel on her own, she was just as nervous as I was!

We arrived in London, at The Whiskey Mist nightclub in Mayfair. I remember seeing all the paparazzi outside because this was the event of the year! The Lava Shells fifth anniversary celebrations were being hosted by a world-famous celebrity magazine at this prestigious venue. A whole host of press, media, celebrities and VIP guests would be arriving shortly, so we were given our instructions on where we would all be working that evening. There were four Lava Angels in total. We would take it in turns to work the dance floor, seating areas as well as the two massage chairs that were centre stage! So, who was on the guest list? The team and I had all been sent emails with the guest list that was completely confidential. I couldn't tell anyone! I remember my stepdaughter being so excited that her stepmum was going to a prestigious event. She had been telling all her friends about her brave stepmum becoming a celebrity therapist! Thing was, I didn't feel brave, I felt I must have been completely nuts to do this! I never ever thought of myself being a celebrity too, that belief didn't actually come until much later.

So many well-known journalists from magazines and newspapers, photographers and celebrities turned up to enjoy the event on such a lovely warm summer's evening. At this point, I was actually starting to feel terrified! But it didn't show, and I didn't falter either. I had decided that I would just treat everyone as if they were my clients. Besides, you know what I found out? Celebrities and media are normal, everyday people just like you and I, but doing extraordinary things. It's their job to be in the limelight. I started to relax, and I found myself really enjoying the event as I chatted to so many different people. I was in uniform, so I was in work mode! I made sure I'd had my roots done and my hair was perfect. Good job too! When I saw the professional photos afterwards, one had homed in right on my scalp! The thing was, I never remembered seeing all the photographers, I just remember focusing on my task of massaging and chatting to the guests, so I wasn't put off by all the flashing lights of the cameras. I was completely switched off to their presence. If I hadn't done so, I would have definitely run out of the main doors when I saw how many photographers and videographers were in the room! This was way out of my comfort zone!

I could feel them all around me, but somehow, I managed to zone out. I had the honour of massaging lots of journalists and one had said she had had a headache beforehand and now it had gone. Plus, she said she had nearly fallen asleep during my massage! Even with all the loud talking and the disco music, I had guests nearly falling asleep on the massage chair from my amazing heated massage… was it me making them relax, not just the Lava Shells? I treated them all as if they were my own clients, making them feel comfortable and performing a full consultation prior to their treatment as well.

I was absolutely buzzing from my first ever celeb event. The paparazzi outside were going wild as we left! "We have to leave now, or we will miss our train home!" I said, sad to leave. It had been a fun event and I will treasure the memory forever.

It wasn't until the next day when I had been tagged by all my friends on social media saying, "Anita OMG have you seen this?" Seen what? Not only was there a picture of me where I had been papped by the world-famous celebrity magazine massaging a celebrity on Twitter, I was also captured on video, which had been streamed live online by a famous London newspaper! I could not believe it! And all the people that didn't believe I would be massaging celebrities had seen the posts, as they all gasped! Well, guess who had the last laugh! I had well and truly started to grow in myself. But there was still a very long way to go.

After this event, I featured in our local newspaper, telling the brief story about what I got up to in London and floods of new clients were contacting me, wanting to try out this amazing new treatment! I had not been prepared for everything that working in the media would bring my way. But I loved it. I loved every minute. And when a huge bouquet of flowers and chocolates arrived from the team, I knew this was it. The start of my celebrity massaging career.

CHAPTER TEN

Never stop getting yourself out there

It was in the summer of 2014 that my dear friend said, "Why don't you have a stall at our school fayre again?" This time it would be in the playing fields, as it was in the height of summer, so I purchased a gazebo and decided on my strategy! I would be performing nail treatments again, as well as promoting myself and my business. But this time I would also be there with my famous Lava Shells. I borrowed my friend's massage chair so that I could perform onsite massages too, as you don't remove any clothes for chair massage. It would be called 'A Love Lava' event.

As I packed up the car, someone said to me, "How do you do it? You've got some guts, you know, I couldn't do what you are doing."

Guts? I was scared stiff yet again! I didn't know if I would gain any more new clients from this event, I just had to embrace the fear. Go out there and do it, and not overthink the process.

'Whether you think you can, or whether you think you can't you are right.'

Henry Ford

I set up my table at the school. It was a lovely warm day with so many mums and dads as well as their children, who had come along to see what was on offer that day. I had ladies come over to see what I was offering. I made some new bookings. One of those new clients still visits me for treatments even now and has stayed very loyal to me. It's tough starting a new business, but you have to get yourself out there. The clients don't come to you, as I had found out the hard way with leaflet drops. There is nothing wrong with this and you do have to try different ways of letting people know about you and what you offer, but in a crowded marketplace, you must stand out from the crowd in order to go the distance and build a reputable, long-term sustainable business.

Personally, I hadn't gained any clients from the leaflet drops. But everything you do is a lesson. And I had found my way to find new clients. By getting myself out there! People buy from people, you don't have to feel brave, you just have to have the guts to go out and do what it takes to get to where you want to be. Stand tall! Be proud of yourself and what you offer. Believe in yourself and others will believe in you, too.

But how do you have guts to do these things when you're scared stiff inside like I was in the beginning? Scared of rejection, scared of messing up. All these feelings are entirely normal and are all part of the process. My advice? You just take a deep breath and trust the process. Don't overthink things. If anything, don't think! Just do it. That's how I managed to conquer my fears. Plus, a lot of positive affirmations reprogramming your subconscious mind. Drown out negative thoughts with meditation. Drown out negative people who say you can't do this. Unfriend if you have to! If you have people laugh at you like I did, make that the fuel to spur you on even more! Then guess who will have the last laugh? You!

I was meant to meet my dear friend, it was as if our paths had crossed for a reason. I am so grateful that she had helped me to get myself up and running with these events at our village school. I will never forget her.

She passed suddenly in October of the same year. She was only forty-four. I was so shocked, as I remember her saying just a few weeks before that she had been having health issues that were being investigated. I was absolutely devastated. My dear friend that I had only known for a short a short time had been taken at such a young age.

The day of the funeral came, and I wasn't going to attend as I was so upset that day, but it was as if I was being called to go. It was as if I needed to say goodbye properly. I wiped my reddened eyes, got dressed and made my way to the church.

The church was packed. She had touched so many hearts with all her love and wisdom, you could feel it all around you. When the reverend spoke of her life and told the story about her father, I then knew I was meant to be there. It was to say goodbye properly to my friend and the deep connection we had shared with both our fathers. I am so grateful for everything she did for me, helping to set up my business, she has left a legacy in my heart forever.

I didn't take part in any more events at the school after that day, it was as if I couldn't bring myself to be there anymore. It was breaking my heart, her smile, her love of life. But the gift she had given me was the power, the drive to go on and do further events, as well as more charity events with the local church. I will never forget her.

That same month I had my next celebrity event to attend. I could not believe it! I was so excited! Me, chosen again? Why me? What makes me special enough to do this important work representing a high-status brand?

"Why not me! Why shouldn't I be chosen? Everyone loves my massages, I am the best! I am a master at my craft. I receive the best testimonials. It is an honour to be chosen!"

I repeated these words to myself in the mirror over and over again. I talked myself into such a positive state that I was actually buzzing by the time I reached my destination. I was working backstage in the booty lounge, which is a marquee backstage at Fusion Festival, held in Birmingham. It was the festival of the year! I could see why my stepchildren loved festivals so much, the atmosphere was electric! Hosted by a national radio station, a whole host of the biggest names in music would be performing at the event. Due to confidentiality, unfortunately I cannot reveal the famous names I had the honour of meeting and massaging that day, but what I can let you in on was that I was asked to massage LIVE on air. The DJ said how amazing my massage was! I was grinning from ear to ear like a Cheshire cat! This, once more, was my moment.

Lava Shell Massage was the most popular treatment on my menu after this event. The local newspaper ran another article about what I did at the event, alongside some photos. I had been so proud to attend and massage at this prestigious venue.

'Daring to be different' was, and has always been, the title for my stories in our local news. I keep a portfolio of all my news articles, as well as celebrity photos, as a reminder of how far I have come. Yet I still have so far to go because life is always a journey.

As I write this book from my heart, as I piece significant moments I've been through together, I can see how some of the events that happened throughout my life have led me up to this point. I used to hide behind my dad when I was growing up! No one would ever have believed me if I hadn't written this book, unless you knew me personally from my youth!

I have written this book especially for you, my reader. The legacy I leave to say to you that no matter where you have come from, what you have been through, your education, or background, you too can make a difference in other people's lives. Because, ultimately, that is why we are here on this planet. To make a difference in other people's lives. It is what keeps us alive and passionate to keep going. You can do it, even if you don't yet believe you can.

"Don't let your past dictate who you are. But let it be a part of who you will become."

Louis Mandylor

CHAPTER ELEVEN

No ordinary girl!

I was being asked to partake in even more celebrity events and I found I had even more new clients requesting appointments! But even though I was getting myself out there more and I was very busy on my therapy days – I even started working in the evening when I came home from my pharmacy days! – I still continued working in both my careers. I worked day and night. Why was this? Well, now as I write this, I can tell you, as I can look back and see what had happened to me along the way on my journey.

I started to believe in myself. I actually believed I could do it! And I was backing up this belief with action! Getting on with what needed to be done to succeed. But a part of me was still holding onto my past. The past that was no longer serving me…

It was my comfort zone.

I wanted to hold onto it so tight as I entered a whole new world. This new world of positive thinking and believing that if you put your mind to it and back the belief with action, you can achieve it! But at times I was so exhausted

I would be ill with colds and headaches again. This wasn't how my life was supposed to be! I had the power within me, I still hadn't reached my full potential yet. It did eventually come, but it was still a long way off as my story continues.

"What did you say?" I was gasping down the phone when I had been asked to perform a pamper party in North London with three other Angels. This was no ordinary pamper party, we had been asked to go to the home of a very famous owner of one of the biggest magazines in the world! Again, I had negative thoughts in my mind! Why me? Why did they choose me? You would think that after performing at all these events I would be supercharged with positivity and excitement! But I wasn't. I was still convincing myself that I wasn't good enough. That I couldn't do this.

"Well, why not me?" What makes me any better than anyone else? Because I had the guts and gumption to go and do it! I felt the fear and said, "YES, I'M IN!" I was so proud of myself.

The thing was, the next major task I had was to ask my manager if I could swap my day of working as it hadn't fallen on my day off! I look back and remember I was actually trembling, thinking I would be laughed at and would be told, 'No, you can't go!' What would your boss say? Can you imagine the scenario?

I was shocked but pleased when my manager said it was fine, but she did look at me in a strange way; it was as if she didn't believe me.

Because of confidentiality like all my events, I cannot tell you who and most importantly where we went for this event. But I can tell you that, to date, it is one of the most glamorous homes I have ever been to. We were working in their spa. Yes! The house had its very own massive spa area.

"Wow!" was all I could say as I stood there looking round the huge room, beside the pool, throwing my arms up into the air! I threw them up with such force, my wedding ring flew right off my finger and into their pool! So, there I was, scrambling down the steps, on my hands and knees in the pool of the owner of a major magazine, frantically trying to fish out my wedding ring! My trousers were soaking wet! The girls all laughed, the housekeeper giggled and just said, "Did you find it?" It was such a funny moment and it actually made us all relax; it was another day I will always remember.

After this event, I trained with a spa skincare brand and from my celebrity work I was asked if I would like to represent them working at a world-class spa. It would be on an ad hoc basis, and it was a real honour, as I found it increased my reputation even further. I loved working at the spa, it was so luxurious and was a real pleasure working with the team. I gained so much more experience as my confidence grew and it gave me lots of new ideas and inspiration for my own business. I carried on working at the spa for a few years, one or two days a month, before finally saying to the company, "Thank you so much for the opportunity but I can no longer offer my time as I am so busy!"

I was also approached and asked to perform massages with Carers4Carers when I first started in my business, a wonderful charity that provides free help, advice and coffee mornings for our unsung heroes who look after their loved ones. I attended this a few times a year, but it was so rewarding emotionally as their hearts and sometimes tears poured out to me as I gave them the gift of touch as I massaged their hands. I am still involved with this charity work, not as much now as my other responsibilities take over, but I will continue to do so when I can as I love helping the carers to feel human again.

*

It was in April 2015 when my friend Sarah and I had the honour of being chosen to massage a famous pop group. The band were touring the country and required the Lava Angels at certain venues to perform Lava Shell back massages to relax them before they went on stage. At the end of the day, we were even escorted to our VIP seats from backstage to watch the show! You should have seen all the fans looking at us, wondering who we were. Sarah and I laughed to ourselves. Never had we ever in our wildest dreams thought when we started our beauty and massage careers that we would be doing this! It wasn't all glamorous, though. When we arrived at our venue, I couldn't find the entrance, so had to drive down a one-way system, hoping I wouldn't receive a ticket! Thirty minutes later, we were about to give up and drive home then I received a call from the manager saying they would wait outside so I could find the entrance. We then had to quickly unload our massage couches and equipment before the fans got to us. Fans got to us? I couldn't stop laughing! Sarah and I were just ordinary massage therapists. Who'd have thought we would be the celebrities too?! "Hurry up and get inside!" the porter had said. "Now you need to go and park your car in the secure car park." This was getting serious, not only did we have to worry about being mobbed by the fans, my car would have been in danger too! Can you imagine this scenario?

Such a different world to the one I was used to, when I was stuck in my comfort zone. Next, we needed to go up to the third floor. The lift only went up to the first floor. We had to lug all our heavy equipment up another two flights of stairs! It was worth it, though, because not only did we massage all the band, but we also got to have our photos taken with them before they went out on stage. Just watching them all prepare to go live… so much work and preparation goes into these events, it's only when you work backstage you get to see all that goes on. It's a real eye opener into another world.

I couldn't sleep that night, I was so hyped up. The photos of us with the band were being splashed around all over social media once again. I was on my way.

My clients were cheering when they saw the photos and my Lava Shell Massage was the talk of the village once more. Another article had gone into our local news… 'DARING TO BE DIFFERENT'.

★

July of 2015, my family and I were out in the Greek islands again, celebrating an important birthday, when I received an email asking if I would like to work at Fusion Festival again in the Autumn. Well, you can imagine what I said! I shrieked and my stepdaughter roared with delight! I felt so honoured and excited because this was the big one I had been waiting for. The biggest and best A-list artists would be performing at this particular event.

Now, had you said to me in 2004 when I had my vision of setting up my own beauty business that I would be massaging A-list music artists, I would have laughed and said, "Don't be so stupid! Me? A pharmacy technician? A beauty therapist?" Well, there I was. I was working backstage once again at Fusion Festival, proudly massaging the stars and being papped with my amazing Lava Shell Massage. I did it.

"If in your heart you believe you can, then you can.
But it's all up to you. No one else."

Anita Swetman

Can you imagine yourself massaging famous people at prestigious locations around the country? So, you may ask yourself, "Why me?" Then say to yourself, "Why not me?"

Me, I was just an ordinary girl in an extraordinary world. But I was no ordinary girl, I was scared, shy, introverted and when I was at school and into my adult life, I was frightened to put my hand up or ask for things in case I looked stupid! Why? Because I really struggled in school as I had learning difficulties in certain subjects. Even if I knew the answer, I had that fear of being laughed at, just incase I was wrong. I lived with fear for so much of my childhood and my adult life. Fear of failure, fear of success. Anxiety would always creep into everything I did. No one ever knew, I hid it well. Only my GP knew when I broke down in his office. I'm so glad I did, or I would still be living in fear now and would never, ever have gone the distance with my career and life now. I would still be waiting for my life to change.

I remember going back to see my doctor a few years later for another ailment and he just looked at me with a great big smile on his face. "You certainly are a different person to the one I saw a few years ago. Well done!"

But it was the events that soon followed that changed my life forever. As if I hadn't been through enough in my life. I could not have prepared myself for what was about to happen next.

CHAPTER TWELVE

I lost myself in action, so I didn't go into despair

"I'm getting remarried, sis!" I couldn't believe it when my brother announced he was getting married for a second time, to the love of his life. The whole family was so happy with this exciting news, and I couldn't wait for their big day!

It was a lovely warm day in September for the wedding, I remember the venue was so beautiful, and it was a perfect location to celebrate their special day. Steve had wanted to honour our father's memory at the occasion, so was dressed in traditional Scottish attire. Kilts, sporran, even the bagpipes were playing. Everything that resembled what our father had loved. Even a three-piece band was present at the wedding breakfast playing all of our dad's favourite songs that we remembered as we were growing up, as our dad used to play double bass and piano when he was in a band many, many years ago. Dad had been entrepreneurial most of his life, I think it's definitely where Steve and I got the bug from.

My brother always loved to make a speech; he would

have made a speech at his own funeral if he could! His speeches always made people laugh and he was always the life and soul of any party. He did, however, also make me cringe sometimes. I had actually forbidden him to make a speech at my wedding, as I just didn't want to be embarrassed by what he might have brought up about my childhood. But this day, his special day, was also a sad one. Not to anyone else, as they would never have known the truth. After all the speeches, my brother sat down at the wedding breakfast table with one of our dad's favourite songs playing in the background and, out of nowhere, Steve suddenly broke down into tears. Not just running down your cheeks tears, but actual sobs. It was then that I knew. I couldn't believe I'd not seen it sooner; he had hidden it so well, just like I had. My mum and I had known my brother longer than anyone in that room and we both knew at that moment, it had all made sense – the kilts, the bagpipes, the three-piece band – Mum and I just looked at each other. Her face started welling up, tears came to my eyes.

Steve was still grieving our father who had died so tragically in 1991. He had never, ever had any form of bereavement counselling or therapy to come to terms with losing Dad. I just couldn't help myself, I felt the pain he showed in his face so deep in my heart, and at that moment I just threw my arms around him and we sobbed together in front of everyone. "It's okay, let it all out. It's been kept inside you for so, so long. I wish you'd confided in me."

"I never told a soul. I wish I'd spoken up sooner," Steve had said to me.

"It's okay, you have now."

If you have ever experienced the sudden death of a loved one, it is so important to seek the help you need to help you get through the trauma. Both Steve and I had let it live on in us for way too long and our health had suffered immensely because of it. Even though we thought we had got through it ourselves. It wasn't until another event came about that it rose right to the surface and reared its ugly head. Always speak to your GP first and they will point you in the right direction for help. You may experience different medication and therapies, but never give up, as you will find the right path to help you heal.

★

It was in April 2018, just over a year and a half since the wedding, when it happened yet again. How many tragedies can one endure in a lifetime to get through in one piece and come out a survivor at the end of the dark tunnel? I'd certainly experienced my fair share of sudden deaths. Could I take yet another one?

I'd been working so hard in my business and my pharmacy career when I took the very brave step to help move my business forward and elevate my status even higher by going in for an award. It was the next stage in my beauty and massage career. When you work from home, no one knows you are there, so you have to work very hard to get yourself out there. But now it was time to go for gold. It was time to shine my light. That ray of light that was beaming out from my heart every single day. I was worthy of this award.

"I'm going for gold!" I announced to all my clients, friends and family on social media. Everyone was so excited, and they were cheering me on. "Go for it, Anita! Wow! An award, how brave are you getting?!" These were some of the comments I was receiving. It's as if they were all waiting to see what I would get up to next! With my celebrity work and now awards, nothing was going to stand in my way of achieving my dream. And so, I visualised winning the gold status of beauty therapist of the year. I put in the work required to win a gold status and gave it my best shot.

The day came when I received an email from the awards team saying that I had been shortlisted for Beauty Therapist of the Year at The British Hair and Beauty Awards. I was working hard to get my portfolio ready to go into round two where the awards team would assess my work, send a mystery shopper to my home therapy room as well as possibly an email or phone enquiry for treatments. I had so much work to do, but I needed to get away from it all. A change of scene. I had run myself ragged and my health was suffering once more. Maybe I had put too much pressure on myself? Did I really need to do this? But something in my heart was telling me I needed to go for the award. As if it was truly meant to be.

My husband and my family packed up the car and travelled up to enjoy a wonderful week in Scotland for Easter in 2018. We all needed the well-deserved break, and we all had a great time away. Everyone had been working so hard and needed the rest. It was on our last day of the holiday that we drove up into the highlands and walked around the beautiful lochs and I was reminiscing about my childhood again. The times I shared there with my family; it was a bit like déjà vu. We visited my dad's favourite loch. The scenery was so beautiful, I stood there for a very long time, looking down the long road that was a gateway to the loch. I always remember being there at that very same spot with my dad when I was young, looking out to the beautiful view together. It was so peaceful and serene, it was a very precious moment in my heart, so I took a photo and sent it to my brother that evening, saying, "Remember this place?" We chatted for a while about the 'good old days', and the things we used to get up to when we were kids, then we said to each other, "See you soon!". We didn't say goodbye.

That was the last time I ever spoke to Steve.

The next morning, we were on our way home with the ten-hour drive back to Warwickshire. We were driving through the Cairngorm mountains when I received the call. The call that I did not know was coming and I did not want to receive.

"No! It's not true!" My head was in a whirlwind, spinning round and round. I refused to believe what I was hearing as I stared at the car phone, I just couldn't take it all in.

The rest of the journey was a blur as I sat there in shock, dazed, shaking. I couldn't even see the mountains anymore. I could feel my body and mind going numb. My stepdaughter in the back of the car put her warm hands on my shoulders and tried her best to comfort me. Thank goodness my husband was driving. Mobile phones are great, but that day, at that very moment in time, I wished I hadn't had mine turned on. I wished I hadn't had my phone with me. I just couldn't take it all in, it must have been a mistake.

It was around ten that Saturday morning, I'd only spoken to Steve twelve hours before! Why? Why? Why?! You just don't know what's round the corner. It had happened once more. I sat there in disbelief. Then my thoughts turned to, "Who's going to tell mum?" My sister was frantically trying to get a flight back from Spain where she lives and couldn't, so it was up to our younger brother to tell our mother the shocking news.

Steve was only forty-nine when he died, so tragically and suddenly. Everyone was in a state of disbelief. Steve had an undiagnosed heart defect. We then all found out that he had been having a series of mini heart attacks in the two weeks before his death that were being investigated. I had phoned into my work to tell them what had happened, and I took the rest of the week off. But, after a few days, I realised I couldn't just stay at home crying, Steve was gone. Nothing would bring him back. It took me a good few days to even speak to anyone, as I was inconsolable. I didn't want to see anyone! But, somehow, I managed to pick myself up and went into work with a very heavy heart after a week, even though I felt like a zombie. My colleagues were surprised to see me back so soon, but I just wanted to keep busy and keep my mind occupied so I didn't wither in despair. I had found it so hard to concentrate, especially when dealing with dispensing medication, I just couldn't do it. I asked my manager if I could stay in the corner of the room and do some work that wasn't too taxing on my exploding brain, and I said nothing about it to anyone. I was crying silently to myself. I was deeply hurting so much inside. My heart was actually aching from the pain. My best friend from when I was young had gone forever from this world. Nothing would bring him back. I cursed myself that I hadn't seen him just a few weeks prior to his death, as we had been busy with another family matter, and this took precedence over seeing my brother. I was beating myself up. But how was I to know this would happen? The only time I could begin to relax and ease my pain was when I was performing treatments on my clients. The pressure of pharmacy and being so busy with treatments, plus going for my awards was starting to take its toll on my health once more. Depression and anxiety reared its ugly head again and I told no one.

"Let us give you more time," the awards team had said to me. I had been working so hard on my portfolio, I worked night and day, then flopped into bed so late at night exhausted so I wouldn't feel any pain. I kept myself so focused on my goal that I didn't have time to grieve. To be sad, to be depressed. No, I refused to let it get the better of me, so I just stayed focused on winning gold. It was the only way I knew how to deal with my feelings, by ignoring them totally. I dumped them into the back of my mind, and I took all focus off my pain as I started to visualise myself winning the gold title. I could actually see myself winning! Nothing – certainly not anxiety or depression – was going to stand in my way!

I submitted my portfolio of evidence to the awards team at the end of April only three weeks after I lost my brother, and it was only a week after the funeral! And then that was it. I had to wait until June. No word, nothing until the day of the awards ceremony.

★

My heart was pounding so loudly, I felt like at any moment it would explode from within me. I knew I didn't have long to wait. The categories were all flashing up online in front of my eyes, I couldn't wait. I was getting so impatient! My heart started pounding louder and louder. It must have seemed like an eternity, then finally they announced my category. Beauty Therapist of the Year.

They always saved the best till last, I guess it's the same as at the Oscars, Best Actress. The biggest and best title of them all! It was at this point I started to doubt myself. Now? Yes! My head was going into overdrive. "You won't even get bronze, you were a fool to enter these awards, you're not good enough. Whatever possessed you to think you, yes you would win gold?" I look back now and realise these last-minute jitters were perfectly normal. But they didn't feel normal to me at the time.

I sat there in utter shock! As tears rolled down my cheeks, it was out there. It just happened. I couldn't believe what I was hearing and seeing. "Well, what's going on?" my husband said, looking at me, seeing me crying my eyes out.

"Woohoo! I've only gone and done it!" I had won the gold title for Beauty Therapist of the Year for East and West Midlands. I was so busy paying attention to my phone that kept on pinging with congratulations messages coming in that I hadn't realised that not only had I won gold, but I had also won the national title!! At first, I thought, 'There must be another Anita Swetman,' but then I saw my picture. A picture of me massaging an A-list celebrity at The Fusion Festival. I could not believe it, but I had envisioned it. I had a vision so strong that I would win gold. And I had backed it up with action and did whatever it took to win that title. But I had never, ever expected to win the national title.

More celebrity work came my way after my awards, I could go on and on about how many celebrities and journalists I've massaged, as well as the amazing venues I've had the honour of working at. It was my dream come true.

When I look deep into my heart, I knew at this point I had truly grown. I had stretched my comfort zone to its maximum limit, and I was starting to move into my growth zone. When you cross that finish line and you win gold too, you will know exactly how it feels and exactly what I mean.

So, what's stopping you from going for gold? I can honestly say, having been through the experience, the only thing stopping you is you. You have the power within yourself even in the darkest moments of your life. You choose whether to let it get the better of you, or you can choose to win.

Chapter Thirteen

Don't wait for a wake-up call to finally take action! Do it now!

Everyone was speechless when they heard that I had won a gold national award. So many people were so happy for me, cheering me on, congratulating me, but one particular person said to me, "It's all right for you, you're full of confidence!" It had cut me to the core. I had known this person for so many years, they knew everything I had been through to get to where I was. They knew I was just an ordinary girl. They really hurt me when their jealousy crept in and said those cruel words. But why be jealous because of someone else's success? You have the power within yourself to go out there and make your own success story! You just don't know unless you try and never give up.

So that was it! Enough was enough! I was sick and tired of being sick and tired.

The strain of working in an environment that was no longer serving my purpose in life, I was heavily grieving my brother and the pain had taken its toll on my health once again. I had started to experience chest pains with anxiety, and it was at this point I finally took action once and for all! But why should it take more wake-up calls to finally take action? Never, ever put things off. You just don't know what's round the corner. Procrastination is the killer of hopes and dreams. I have truly learned the hard way, but it was all an experience and part of my learning curve.

*

It was a bank holiday in 2018 and I was at lunch when all of a sudden I experienced chest pains and flashing lights came over one of my eyes. The side of my face had started to go numb, it travelled down right to my jaw, and it was getting worse. I truly was frightened! What was happening to me? I could no longer hide it. "Can you get me some help please, I'm not sure if I may be having a stroke," I said anxiously to my colleague. My boss flew up the stairs into the canteen. "At this moment your face isn't drooping, can you raise your arm? I've called 999 for assistance."

Thank goodness my face wasn't drooping. I was so scared but retained my composure and tried to stay calm. The emergency services had said I needed to get to hospital straight away, but it would be quicker for me to make my own way there than wait for an ambulance due to the bank holiday madness of people in town and traffic chaos.

My husband came straight away, picked me up and we got to our local A&E as fast as we could. It was a very hot day and, as I sat there in the waiting room, tears welled up in my eyes thinking of how my brother and my father must have been so scared, alone and afraid the day they left us all forever.

As I write this paragraph in my garden on a warm Saturday morning, I have to keep stopping as my tears continue to flow and stop me from seeing my screen as I transport myself back to what happened that day. The day that changed my life forever. I regain my composure, meditate and then carry on with my story to you.

It seemed like an eternity waiting to be seen by the doctor. Bank holidays are not good days to be sitting waiting for assistance in A&E! Our national health service is wonderful and we are so lucky to have it.

It seemed a very long time, but in fact I was only there ten minutes before I was ushered into the doctor's office to be examined. When you're stressed and anxious, time seems to slow down, and you feel as if you will never get through it.

To my relief, I was diagnosed with experiencing an optical migraine, which had been brought on by extreme stress. My chest pains were anxiety. I couldn't believe it. My grief had been eating away at me inside and now it had reared its ugly head with these symptoms. This was it, this was my final wake-up call. A final warning that my body had given me that now I needed to take action or else I would end up like my dad and my brother.

That very day, I made the biggest decision of my life, aside from getting married. I wasn't going to go back to being that frightened little girl who was afraid to make something of her life and remain stuck in a career that wasn't her calling. Don't get me wrong, I gave my all to my career, but after being on the same path since I was eighteen, it was time to move on.

I had a lot to think about on holiday in the summer regarding my future there, it was time for me to make a stand. It was time to finally call it a day. It was time to get well and truly out of my comfort zone! It was time for me to go fully self-employed.

No more procrastinating, hanging onto a career 'just in case' my beauty career failed, this was it. No going back. I am going to make it work! The decision had been made. When I went back to work in August, I was going to hand in my notice, ending nearly seventeen years' employment at this particular branch.

I slept soundly after we had made the decision together, my husband and I. At long last, I was able to relax and switch off to really enjoy the rest of my holiday and, when I went back to work the following Monday, I left the envelope with my resignation on my manager's desk. I felt nervous. I had held onto the envelope tightly in my hands. I closed my eyes and said to myself, "This is it, just put it there," and then I closed the door behind me without looking back.

My boss was shocked, but not surprised. I had given a fair three months' notice to fill my position; I only needed to give a month, but I wanted to be honest and let them know that I had to leave for the sake of my health, as well as my sanity. "Please think seriously before leaving your career behind." I know my boss didn't want me to leave,

I was a very valued member of the team and I had been told by a senior member that most people when they leave don't give a damn about their work, "But you did," she said to me. I think I cared too much, but that's me! I give everything my all in life. Even if it doesn't serve me anymore. Because that was how I got through things. To give my all and be the very best I could be.

There is no room in this world to be stuck in something you don't want to do anymore, you either give it your all or you leave, it's your choice.

I had a lovely leaving meal with some of my friends from work, it was a wonderful, yet sad occasion, as they handed me my leaving gifts they had all clubbed together for. They had all touched my heart in so many ways and I cried that they were actually sad to see me go. "I will miss you all, but I have to live my life on my terms."

I finally walked out of those doors for the last time on the 31st of October 2018. This was it. No turning back!

On the 5th of November 2018, I went full time in my beauty and massage career. I'd had a part-time income from my self-employment up until this stage, but how on earth was I going to make it full time? "This is it, you can do this! You can make your part-time business into a full-time one." YES, I CAN! If it's going to be, it's up to me! No one else.

"I am in control of my own destiny! No one else"
Anita Swetman

I put my heart and soul into making my business full time. I'd had a beautiful new website designed for me just a few years before, so now it was time to get it out there further by posting onto social media, making the big announcement that I had now increased my hours for clients to book in for treatments. Before I knew it, I had clients from a few years earlier saying, "That's brilliant! Now I can come to you on my day off!" and "I can now start telling my friends!" Before I knew it, my diary had very quickly filled up and I had doubled my income! Yes, I literally doubled my income in that first month. But it didn't just come to me, I went to them. I got myself out there telling everyone that I had increased my hours once more.

It wasn't easy filling up my diary, I had some no shows, clients cancelling at the last minute, and I would let them off! Well, not anymore! I had terms and conditions on my website but now it was time to put them into force!

I give clients a 'three strike system'. So, basically, if they cancelled their appointments three times then I would ask for full payment upfront. All new clients were to pay a 50% non-refundable booking fee so then I could eliminate the time wasters. If clients are genuinely ill, you have to be flexible. But I always asked if they wanted to reschedule and nine times out of ten they did.

I always ask clients after their appointment if they would like to rebook, and the majority always do. That was how I built up my regular clientele. The personal service I provide to all my clients is what won me my awards and I pride myself in my work.

I also charged my worth! After winning a gold national status and massaging celebrities, investing in the finest products, my education and ongoing continual professional development, I performed to stay on top of my game, being there for my clients when they required advice, when they needed me out of working hours, I certainly wasn't going to skimp on my prices! But I also keep them affordable.

It was the best December I had ever had, and this was the first year in a very long time that I actually looked forward and was excited about working at Christmas. I worked my full-time career around my husband's shift pattern, so that when clients arrived, they never felt like they were intruding on personal space, and they loved that. I had created a relaxing home-from-home experience. I was able to take the same holidays as my husband and my clients were happy that they could plan all their treatments around my me time. Each month was going so well, even in January and February when most businesses are quiet. Everyone wants something to look forward to, and my services were just what my ladies were looking for. Yes sure, I had some empty spaces, but I had replaced my pharmacy income, so in that respect I felt truly fulfilled and successful. I always embraced the pause to have some downtime. You must always remember to look after yourself too or else you will be no good to anyone!

★

I popped in to see my colleagues that Christmas, taking them a big box of chocolates, as I knew that would go down well with them. They had said how much younger I looked! Someone said to me, "I wish I was brave enough to do what you have done." I looked her straight in the eye and said, "There is no difference between you and me, I just made the decision to change my life and I backed it with action. If you really want to change your life you can." That was it!

I was loving my new life. Our marriage was strong, and I found my husband was so much happier when he came home from work each day. It was as if he had his wife back. I guess I didn't realise how much of a strain my work had put on us.

★

In June 2019, I won the gold title once more for Beauty Therapist of the Year, but this time it was for a much wider area, covering the Midlands, Southwest and Wales. Yet again, I had visualised winning the gold title. I kept myself focused on my goal and did the work and what it took to win the title. I looked back at the previous year and what I was going through at the time of going for my awards. I thought about how far I had come, yet still had so far to go, as life is always a journey, never a destination.

CHAPTER FOURTEEN

When the odds are against you, you have a choice which path to take

It was the beginning of March in 2020, which was another important turning point in my life, as I had made the bold, brave decision to train in derma cosmeceutical skincare. Some of my clients had skin issues that my current skincare line was no longer helping them with, so I had to go and do some deep research into finding alternative ways to aid my clients with their skin issues. It wasn't easy, as there are so many products on the market. Then I finally found what I had been looking for!

I took some time off work and travelled to South Wales for my skin health training. I can do that now, I'm the boss of me! No one to answer to but myself! When you are self-employed, you are in control of your own choices and your own destiny.

I booked the time out in my diary and had decided to make a girly weekend of it as one of my therapist friends had decided she wanted to train with this company too.

I made the big announcement on social media as I

checked into our hotel, and the comments from clients came flooding in! "Good luck, I can't wait to try the new skincare line and see the results with my skin."

I found at first the concept of how derma cosmeceuticals work in the skin confusing, but my skin tutor had been a science teacher and a chemist before embarking on a beauty career and she explained it so well. I was absorbing my newfound knowledge like a sponge and was hungry for more education. I loved learning, then being able to share what I had learned with my clients and help them further with their skin. I just couldn't wait to launch these amazing, wonderful products and skin treatments.

As a professional therapist, ongoing continual professional development is essential to stay ahead of the game. If you want to stand out in this crowded marketplace in beauty and spa, you need to be different and offer a unique, bespoke service like no other.

Always research your products thoroughly. I made a couple of costly mistakes with products along my journey, but I made sure I learned from those experiences. It really is trial and error, finding what works best for you and your clients. I highly recommend professional exhibition shows, as you can experience first-hand new products and services, as well as networking with the companies directly to see if they may be a good fit for your business, no matter what industry you are in.

★

On 7th of March 2020, alongside three other amazing therapists, as well as volunteers, I held yet another afternoon tea and pamper event, which we had been planning for the last three months. I planned to launch my new skincare line on the day, and we all worked hard to get the event ready.

With the help of everyone, I held the best, most successful charity event I had ever done! So many ladies came up to me saying how much they had enjoyed the afternoon. The event had been combined with a fashion show and the tickets sold out! Most of my clients attended the event, as well as a few new ladies who still come for treatments today.

That was how I did it. I got myself out there once again with the people. Always remember: Regular, loyal clients don't come to you, you always go to them! They warm to your personality. Show yourself and give the best of yourself. No matter how you are feeling. And now, after all my years of hard work getting myself out there with stalls, charity pamper events, celebrity events, new clients come and find me. I'd worked so hard to build up my reputation and my service that now they were booking and rebooking treatments with me. Ladies started talking to their friends and I received more new bookings through word-of-mouth recommendations.

I even set up a couple of VIP client groups on Facebook so that I could post last-minute availability, as well as exclusive offers for ladies. I decided on a dedicated skincare group where I post advice and tips on getting the most out of home care products, as well as being their personal dedicated skin specialist. I also have a group for other treatments that I offer so clients can choose which group they would like to belong to. When I have a new client book in, I always ask them how they heard about me so I can monitor what's working well. I have to say, my website designer makes sure I am always top ranking on Google, it is working really well and saves me so much time as I delegate the responsibility to her. I also send email campaigns to clients that sign up for exclusive news, and schedule in my social media posts so I don't have to worry about what to post.

This was how I built my business. From November 2018 until the end of March 2020, I had completed my first full year and a half being fully self-employed.

That was when my door closed to my clients alongside so many other businesses. Just like that, overnight. I was no longer allowed to treat the public. The Covid-19 virus was upon us all over the world and close contact services were deemed as 'non-essential'.

I went into a whirlwind of emotions. "I can't believe it!" I cried. I'd put my heart and soul into my passion. I'd just completed my first full year of self-employment on my tax return then it was all gone. Just like that! Another wake-up call! How many wake-up calls can one endure in their lifetime?

However, this was a different kind of wake-up call. I had no income whatsoever. I had kept my eggs all in one basket with only one form of income now I'd left my pharmacy career behind, so I was effectively out of work. Everything I had worked hard for, for so many years, had been taken away from me, just like that. How was I going to pay my share of the bills? I had left my other career on faith to build my business full-time, but I couldn't go back and ask for work! Why not, Anita? Well, because once you make the decision to move forward, there is no going back! There was no way I was going to go back to an hourly wage when I had learned how to control my own income. I didn't want to rely on my husband to help me pay all the bills either! I was going to pay my own way. I am strong and I am a fighter, and I knew, somehow, I would get through this! I would find a way to have money coming in without going out again and getting a job! "I can do this!"

It took me a few days to get my thoughts back on track again. I needed to meditate and calm my mind, so I could see clearly though the storm as I, like so many others, was 'grieving' the temporary loss of my business. How long would I be closed for? No one knew how long we would be in lockdown. This virus had taken over the world so quickly and it was just like something from the movies! You never, ever expect it to happen in real life! I did manage to regain my self-control, and I started to think straight again. I started saying positive affirmations to myself.

"You can get through this. Winners never quit! With all that you have been through in your life up to this point, no global pandemic is going to put you out of business!"

I felt better, uplifted and ready to perform a video for my

VIP client group explaining how I was feeling and letting them all know I was still here, even though I couldn't let them into my home for their much-loved treatments. I took a deep breath and recorded a video.

I had received so many lovely private messages from my clients that my heart ached. Tears rolled slowly down my cheeks upon reading some of the most heartfelt messages I had ever read. They all cared so much about me, as I did for them. We all had such a strong bond. This was what I had put into my business. I always treated my clients as if it was their first ever visit every single time. They were all treated like they were my family.

The next night, I had a dream, a vision so strong about how I could earn an income whilst in lockdown. I visualised performing online skin consultations with my clients and then recommending the products for home care use. I was safely delivering them to their door! Was this possible? Would I even be allowed to do this? As soon as I woke the next day, I didn't waste another minute. The time was now to take action! I very quickly posted on my skincare therapist stockist group about the dream I'd had and asked if they thought it was a crazy idea. I never thought for one minute that they would laugh at me, as so many therapists posted saying, "What a fantastic idea!"

To my surprise, my skincare company came back to me saying this is what they had been planning as soon as the government had made the announcement about locking down the country. I could not believe it! They already had this in motion for all of us therapists. The devotion and support they gave us was second to none. I then knew I was meant to train and invest with this company.

> "Trust in your visions and your dreams, they are a calling to something greater."
>
> *Anita Swetman*

The following week, we had a plan given to us with ongoing continual professional development that would be fed to us daily, plus a whole session dedicated to how to perform an online skin consultation with a client. I embraced the challenge and kept the faith that I could do this, I believed in myself so much. I had this burning desire deep inside my heart to go the distance, so I would be able to start recommending skincare online to my clients. It wasn't easy and it took a while to get it all up and running as this whole new way of online selling was so alien to me. But if you are willing to be a student, open to the possibilities that are out there and set your mind to it, as well as backing it with action, you can then go on to achieve it!

> "What if I fall? Oh, but my darling, what if you fly?"
>
> *Erin Hanson*

The commission I earned each month in product sales was just about enough to keep my head above water with paying my share of our bills. But it wasn't enough. I had also invested and taken part in a couple of boot camps to learn how to market online, so I could make sure I upped my game and be the very best once again for my clients.

One day at the end of June, one of my friends put up a post on Facebook saying she was looking for people to join her in her network marketing company. This was not something I had planned to do, as I had done this type of selling many years before when my late brother had introduced me to the concept, and I had quit because I'd hardly made any money. But back then that was because I didn't believe in myself. Now I did! I had grown stronger and stronger with each passing year! What I had achieved in my life up to this point was testament to this. I signed up to the business opportunity, as it was free to join, and I started selling the products online – with the help of my friend – to my clients, as well as new customers. The products were amazing value for money. My customers loved them, and wonderful reviews were coming in. I even started to grow a team, as my excitement grew and my newfound career was taking off. It was certainly helping to keep the bills paid and to this day I am so truly grateful for that business. But it wasn't my calling to go back into network marketing, even though I love the products and I still use them.

Now the lockdowns have ended and finally I'm back to work with my passion, I no longer had the inclination in building another team and managing them. That's not what I wanted to do. It wasn't my path. It served its purpose whilst I had no other money coming in, and my customers can still order from me if they wish, as I will always keep my web shop open. I am always there to help and support those in my team if they need me, as I love helping others achieve in life.

As I continue to write my first ever memoir in June 2021, I'm back to a 'new' normal, treating my wonderful clients in my home salon. But now I'm on the floor with my clients just four days a week, with alternate weeks of working just the mornings, then the following week afternoon and evenings, so I can have a balance in my life while earning a full-time income. With the skincare product sales still coming in each month, I can now afford to regain more time in my life and that has given me the opportunity to write this book especially for you, my reader, and focus on my writing career with more books for you to read in the future.

But it wasn't easy to get going again, opening up my home to clients after we came out of lockdown. I was full of anxiety when the prime minister had said we could open close contact services again. The first lockdown was tough, then being back to work in the August, then another month of lockdown in November, I felt like a yo-yo. The new year from January until mid-April was definitely the hardest lockdown ever, which I'm sure was very hard for so many. Cold dark nights, being shut in and only being able to go out for a walk. I couldn't even begin to imagine what people who were already suffering with their mental health could be going through at this point. But, actually, I could. You see, in the first lockdown I was unable to get any online delivery slots from the supermarket we used.

So, we had to go out to the supermarket! My anxiety was rife queuing up with my mask on. It had taken quite a few weeks before I could go there on my own. But I did it! I pushed through the fear of catching Covid and stayed safe when I shopped for groceries.

It was tough building up to get back to normality with treatments, as well as the trust aspect my clients had in me to keep them safe. When my most vulnerable clients started to come back after so long, they stopped me in my tracks when I was explaining my safety procedures, saying, "Anita, I have always felt safe with you." That made my heart melt, and I knew all my hard work had been worth it.

Life is a journey, it's this roller coaster of events that have led me to where I am today writing this book for you, my reader. It was this worldwide virus that then led me to meet a stranger online that became my friend and helped me with my new calling of how to become an author.

Cassandra Farren had posted about a free five-day boot camp on social media she was holding on elevating your authority. How did I know about this? I just happened to go onto Facebook that day and it came up in my newsfeed. I read all about what would happen on this challenge, and what it could lead to. I love challenges, as you now know, having read most of my story! And something deep inside my heart was saying, "You need to join this!" But why was I joining in five days of challenges to become an author when I'm now back to fulfilling my calling of being a therapist?

"It's in the moments of decision that your destiny is shaped."

Anthony Robbins

CHAPTER FIFTEEN

The Secret...
are you living your dream?

In April 2021, just before lockdown ended, I was at a low point again in my life, with my mood being great one day then down the next. The uncertainty of whether I could get back to my passion was in the balance. Everyone was eagerly waiting for lockdown to end. It seemed like an eternity.

I had heard about the book called *The Secret* but I had never read it. Then I saw there was a documentary on TV about the book and I watched it one afternoon. I could not believe it! I watched it three more times back-to-back! I had nothing else to do, I was still effectively out of work, apart from my online selling and education. As I watched and absorbed what I was seeing and hearing, I sat there stunned! It suddenly dawned on me that I had been living my dream! The dream I visualised back in 2004 of setting up my own business and the vision I had in my mind every day of making it all a success had come true!

I sat there in awe as I looked back over the years at

what it took to get me to this point today. Everything I had gone through, I hadn't even realised that I was using 'The Law of Attraction' every single day. It was my calling and I had embraced the challenge. I had gone through so much to achieve my dream! I slept so peacefully that night, the best night's sleep I'd had in nearly four months. Even though I had been closed down temporarily due to Covid restrictions, I was in fact living my dream.

It was in mid-April, only a couple of weeks after I'd watched *The Secret*, when Cassandra announced she was holding her challenge on Facebook on how to become an author. Something deep inside was telling me that I should join this group as it just felt right, as if I had been called to take part in the journey.

I was very eager to start the challenge and on day one I met some amazing first-time authors in the group. I completed the challenges every day and made sure I was present for when Cassandra went live in the group each day. Before I knew it, at the end of day five, I had in fact written the first 3000 words of my book! I could not believe it! Neither could anyone else in the group! All I did was trust that this was my path to take, even if I did not yet know it. So, I kept on writing...

I've found becoming an author has come very naturally to me. It definitely was as if it was meant to be. I was led onto this path and then, before I knew it, I was over 12,000 words into my book writing journey within just three weeks! This book you are reading right now! The whole group of members were in awe of what I had achieved, cheering me on! I also found it was one of the most uplifting groups I had ever belonged to, and it felt right conversing with my newfound first-time author friends and we motivate and uplift each other to keep on keeping on.

I have now come to the end of my memoir on 7th of August 2021. So how did I achieve that in just over three months? It's no secret, I just kept on going. I believed in myself and my story so much. I just wanted to keep on writing. I was motivated, driven and I did not procrastinate and put it off like I did all those years ago. When I could have been sitting watching TV, or out having a great time, I was writing my memoir when my husband was fast asleep from having started work so early in the morning.

So, there I was, sitting in my garden listening to the birds with my iPad late into the evening, just writing without stopping until I could write no more that day. It wasn't easy, though. There were times I just didn't know the right words to say, so I would meditate again and put my hand on my heart and ask for the correct words to flow. I experienced physical pain in my heart and stomach on certain aspects of my memoir, as I delved deep within my soul to tell you my story. But I did it and I embraced the challenge!

The time is now. Why wait? Tomorrow is not promised. Just three months ago I joined Cassandra Farren's writing academy to learn how to become an author. I just got on with what needed to be done to complete my memoir. I performed my author meditations every single day and always before I wrote, so that my words would flow out freely from my heart onto my page.

I truly believe that once you come out of your comfort zone, that feeling of being safe, you then start to push through the fear zone as you try new things, then onto your learning zone into your growth zone. And that is where the magic truly happens. When the odds are against you and you need to earn a further income, you open your mind and your heart to what is possible. Getting a job with an hourly wage is not an option anymore. Why build someone else's dream when you could be building your own and your family's dreams?

When you work for yourself, you are in control. No one else. You are in the driving seat, and you are the boss! You will, however, need to possess a few qualities, but this is not an exhaustive list that follows. You will need to be self-motivated, self-disciplined, driven, ambitious, have a burning desire to change your life, be open to exploring new opportunities and, most importantly, become a student again!

You don't need a business degree, you don't need lots of money to start up! And age is never, ever a factor.

I was always told having your own business was not for the faint-hearted. Well, as I write this now and you have read through my story, you can see that I was faint-hearted at times, but I did it! I pushed through my fears to make a difference in mine as well as other people's lives. Take the focus off yourself to help others. Then you will become the person you dream of becoming, no matter what career path you choose!

I chose to become a beauty therapist, but no ordinary

beauty therapist! And now I'm also becoming an author. As I embark on my new writing career, I have dreams and visions for further books, as my heart is leaning towards fiction storytelling. But I think I may just have to write non-fiction too! What do you think my next book will be about? I would love to hear your ideas.

I hope you enjoyed reading my memoir, certain events leading my path to where I am today.

If I can help one person, just one person believe that they too can achieve whatever they put their mind to and back it with action, then I am a huge success.

I want to see you fly too! I would love for you to come back to me and tell me how my book has helped you and how far you flew!

Anita x

"Do not allow the ghosts from your past to steal the happiness of your future."

Cassandra Farren

A poem from one of Anita's clients:

If ever you feel in need of some TLC,
Tranquil Beauty is the place to be.
Anita's warm welcome will put you at ease,
With her smile, wise advice, she's ready to please.
So it is no surprise to those who know her kindness and
care,
That her gold-star achievement was won fair and square.
We're more than happy to celebrate and raise a glass of
good cheer!

Chris Murphy

Contact Anita

To find out more about Anita please visit her website:

https://www.anitaswetman.com

You can connect with Anita on social media:

www.facebook.com/anitaswetmanofficial
https://www.facebook.com/tranquil1beauty
Instagram : @anitaswetmanauthor
Twitter : @AnitaSwetman
https://www.linkedin.com/in/anita-swetman-author/

For speaking or press enquiries, please email:

anitaswetman@btinternet.com

Anita would love you to leave a review for *No Ordinary Girl* on Amazon.

Available in paperback and Kindle from Amazon and other major retailers.

Acknowledgments

I would firstly like to say thank you to my husband for always supporting me when I made the decision to change my career. For All the nights we spent apart whilst I was studying hard to achieve my new qualifications to enter a different world. Thank you for believing in me that I could make my business the success it is today. You are my rock. Always have and always will be.

My father in spirit. Your strength and wisdom have helped me grow into the butterfly I am today. The entrepreneurial spirit you always had and your holistic approach to life, I live and breathe every day and now they have shone into the strong woman I am today.

My brother Stephen in spirit. If you hadn't have introduced me to my very first business opportunity and the power of positive thinking when I was twenty three, I would never have achieved everything I have up to this day. I would never have met my husband. You are with Dad now, may both of your entrepreneurial spirits live on in me forever.

I would like to thank all my clients, past and present. You are the glue that has made my beauty and massage business the success it is today, growing stronger by the minute. Without you, it would cease to exist.

To Clare, I thank you for giving me the amazing opportunity to be able to work at so many prestigious events massaging some of the greatest people in the media and show business. It has helped me to grow as a person and taken my business to new heights I never could have dreamed of.

To my dear friend. Our paths crossed for a reason and I thank you for all your help in launching my business with events. If we hadn't have parked our cars in the same place each day, we never would have made the connection.

To Cassandra. Our paths crossed on social media for a reason. I was meant to write this book, I trusted that this was my path. I embraced the journey and took my entrepreneurial spirit to the highest level possible.

Thank you for all your help and guidance in the writing academy and with my book writing journey.

To Jen. I would like to say a very big thank you for your guidance and support in the editing, designing and publication of my book. Whenever I needed advice you always replied with a very positive, cheerful email. For a first time author learning all the time, I knew my manuscript was in very safe hands.

To my mum, my brother and my sister. I know I have shocked you with all I have achieved in my life, I'm looking forward to shocking you some more!

3987841UK00007B/320
UKHW021901150222
Milton Keynes UK
Lightning Source UK Ltd.